Praising
Gregor T. Goethals
The Electronic Golden Calf

"Gregor Goethals persuasively makes the argument that the popular media construct and shape the images that constitute our life. I wonder if we are prepared to exercise that awesome task responsibly."

—SEAN COLLINS
Associate Producer, National Public Radio

"A chilling, insightful analysis of television's construction of our sense of reality by a leading artist and art critic."

—SALLIE McFAGUE
Vanderbilt University

"Mésalliance or ideal union? Sacrilege or blessing? A fascinating and provocative study of the relationship between high art and low. An unprecedented investigation of popular images of the media as the generative force of a new theology, morality and aesthetic in art."

—DAVID SHIREY
School of Visual Arts, New York

THE
ELECTRONIC
GOLDEN
CALF

ALSO BY GREGOR GOETHALS

The TV Ritual: Worship at the Video Altar

THE
ELECTRONIC GOLDEN CALF

■ ■ ■

IMAGES, RELIGION, AND THE MAKING OF MEANING

GREGOR T. GOETHALS

COWLEY PUBLICATIONS
Cambridge, Massachusetts

Published in the United States of America by Cowley Publications, a division of the Society of St. John the Evangelist. No portion of this book may be reproduced, stored in or introduced into a retrieval system, or transmitted, in any form or by any means, including photocopying without the prior written permission of Cowley Publications, except in the case of brief quotations embodied in critical articles and reviews.

Library of Congress Number: 89-78008

Library of Congress Cataloging-in-Publication Data
Goethals, Gregor T., 1926
   The electronic golden calf: images, religion, and the making of meaning / Gregor T. Goethals.
      p. 225 cm.
   Includes bibliographical references.
   ISBN 1-56101-007-3 (alk. paper) : $21.95
   ISBN 1-56101-002-2 (pbk. : alk. paper) : $11.95
   1. Image (Theology) 2. Television in religion—United States.
I. Title.
BV 652.97.U6G64 1990
246—dc20   89-78008
                                                  CIP

This book is printed on acid-free paper and was produced in the United States of America.

Cowley Publications
980 Memorial Drive
Cambridge, Massachusetts 02138

ACKNOWLEDGMENTS

Ideas presented here first took shape in a workshop organized by the Society of St. John the Evangelist, and since then I have been privileged to work with Cynthia Shattuck, the director of Cowley Publications, to complete this book.

From the beginning it was clear that these ideas needed to be examined in an interdisciplinary context. I am very grateful to Robert W. Lynn and the Lilly Endowment for their interest in the arts and theological education. Their support allowed the dialogue to proceed first at Andover-Newton Theological School, where I benefitted from work and conversations with Gabe Fackre and Max Stackhouse, and then at Yale University as part of a team exploring the arts in theological education. Exchanges there with colleagues John Cook, Peter Hawkins, and David Kelsey were very productive, and I am especially indebted to George Lindbeck for his suggestions.

Friends and colleagues at Rhode Island School of Design have been supportive in countless ways. Susan Ward and Don Keefer went over the final draft with me in great detail, while Hammett Nurosi graciously agreed to help with the cover design.

At the heart of a support system are those who know what's going on with the computer. Helen Moffatt painstakingly transferred the manuscript to the word processor, while Margaret Lewis worked through editorial changes and additions with meticulous care; her skill and interest in the final stages were invaluable. I owe thanks as well to my brother, John Thompson, who patiently instructed me in the use of the computer.

From beginning to end, John F. Wilson has been exceedingly generous in his support of the project and his willingness to critique material, while Virginia Clifford is the one to whom I have repeatedly turned to try out ideas. Her critical editorial eye, insight, and encouragement over the years have contributed immeasurably to this work.

Finally, I am grateful to Sean Collins, Gordon Kaufman, Sallie McFague, and David Shirey for their careful reading and helpful comments.

TABLE OF CONTENTS

CHAPTER FOUR

THE MAKING OF MEANING   159

SELECTED BIBLIOGRAPHY   213

THE
ELECTRONIC
GOLDEN
CALF

INTRODUCTION

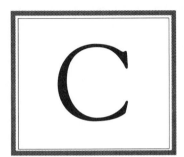ontemporary artists who are interested in spirituality generally explore religious symbols in isolation, and many reject the liturgical settings, myths, and uses of the arts in churches and synagogues. For some, the practice of art has become a form of private meditation, and appreciative viewers go to the museum for inspiration, wonder, and contemplation. At the same time, the arts we generally call "popular," like television, have taken over a major role that visual images historically performed: the public communication of shared beliefs. Like traditional religious art, the mass media present symbols of authority and portray common values. In both high and popular culture artists construct visual meanings, attempting in various ways to render visible invisible truths which illuminate experience. In contemporary society this impulse has found extensive expression outside the church.

This book is an attempt to understand the transformation and dispersal of the sacramental functions of images in a secular and pluralistic society. To explore this concern I have selected from certain historical periods illustrations which show both the impulse to construct world views in visual terms and the fragility of such constructions. I do not attempt to present a "history." Instead, I have sought to make exploratory incisions into cultural history at key points that offer perspectives on the roles of contemporary high and popular art in the creation of religious meaning.

Each chapter attempts to frame particular questions and to highlight changing attitudes about the communication of religious meanings. The connecting thread is a concern for the role of the image maker in the construction of a world, in the embodiment of values and beliefs so that they are accessible to ordinary persons. My principal interest is in the contrasting sacramental roles that high and popular art play: the private worlds of meaning shaped by "Art" and the pervasive environment of commonplace symbols created by television in American society.

Since I find analogies for these dual roles in the functions of religion, it seemed important to begin with a brief look at Judeo-Christian attitudes towards the visual arts and the tensions between the Greek and Hebraic traditions. This antithesis between the iconic and aniconic aesthetic has reverberated through western culture well into the present. While the use of images in world religions is commonplace, some traditions have tended to exclude the representational arts, particularly in the liturgical setting. In the first chapter I have drawn out the dialectic between these two aesthetics. The biblical rejection of images was unique in Mediterranean culture, where the visual portrayal of myths and world views was widespread, yet over time artisans appropriated the visual language of the late classical world to narrate sacred stories and enhance ritual spaces. Eventually the use of images for instruction and the nurture of faith became commonplace in western Christianity.

Yet conflicting attitudes about the use of images did not disappear, and beneath the surface, always ready to erupt, lay an iconoclastic impulse. We shall see how contrasting views about images resulted in both an iconic and an aniconic aesthetic in Christendom. These existed side by side in the twelfth century, articulated by two extraordinary churchmen—Suger, Abbot of St. Denis and Bernard of Clairvaux. Later, sixteenth-century reformers—especially Calvin and Zwingli—radically changed attitudes about images and their use in worship. Churches following their principles were emptied of painting and sculpture, and artists, once supported by religious institutions, began looking for other opportunities and new symbols. In Protestant countries changing roles for art and artists began to emerge, bringing new patrons and a diversity of subject matter—landscape, genre, still-life portraiture. Artists particularly concerned with religious motifs often continued to represent biblical subjects, but in countries influenced by the radical reformers, the churches found no place for them.

In the second chapter the focus moves to the New World, where we will look at the construction of religious symbols in a democratic society—the United States. Without the traditional patrons of art—church and state—there was no institutional support for the creation of visual public symbols. American artists in search of religious meaning were on their own, and in this vacuum they began to explore images that could communicate the beliefs and values of the new democracy and to seek a special public role for the artist. Nature was an important symbol for understanding a creating, ordering God who had guided a special people to a New Eden. For a few artists—who wrote as well as painted—nature had a special power to evoke religious sentiment. To Asher B. Durand, a landscape painting could, even without biblical narrative, communicate a religious truth. Yet, as an *icon*, landscape depends very much upon the religious sensibilities of painters and viewers. In the twentieth century, the spiritual searches of some artists led them away from all representational imagery to non-objective art.

Wassily Kandinsky and Piet Mondrian laid the foundations early in the twentieth century for what became a new idiom for mid-century artists concerned with religious meaning. While for many the formal concerns of abstract art were paramount, others saw themselves as new mythmakers. For painters like Mark Rothko and Barnett Newman, the making of art became an individual spiritual odyssey. For Paul Tillich a number of mid-century artists, through their encounter with meaninglessness, expressed a religious "courage to be." Now, at the end of the century, "art" itself has taken on an aura of the sacred. It is a commodity treasured as a relic, and in a secular society the artist is often revered as shaman and mystic.

The museum offers meditative objects and quietness for reflection. But once out on the streets, or before the TV set, we are caught up in other kinds of sacramental images: tales of the good life, the happenings at the boundaries of our "world," and the political icons of those who lead it.

The third chapter turns from high art to popular culture, especially television. As the fine arts of the twentieth century moved deeper into the private visions of individual artists, the power and responsibility for the communication of shared, public meanings have been taken over by the popular arts. Pervasive print and electronic media have for decades expressed and celebrated the values of a secular society. The technological revolution in image-making sparked an encompassing sacramental revolution. As in the past, contemporary institutions—political and economic—have come to depend upon images to give concrete expression to tenets of faith that are as authoritative in our own day as the Parthenon friezes were for the citizens of fifth-century Athens. Arts generally considered inferior or commercial now perform functions similar to those of monumental arts of previous cultures. Today the artists of popular culture, like medieval craftsmen, fashion images to communicate the beliefs that define our world. Like those revered stained glass windows or carved statuary of earlier times, the elusive representations of TV depict a mythological framework for contemporary individual and collective life, for the American Way.

In today's world the aesthetic and religious imagination of the church—understood in all its pluralistic, denominational forms—has been challenged by two aspects of secular creativity. The expression of shared public meanings and values has been taken over by the popular arts, especially by television, while

the view of high art as a source of personal meaning has transformed the making of art into a saving experience. Both artists
and viewers construct meanings and myths independent of religious institutions. The last chapter will consider the nature of
these challenges and how churches may respond to them. Have
religious institutions become so closely identified with the
values of the good life portrayed on television that they have
lost sight of their own distinctive symbols? Have the traditional
symbols of denominations become so lackluster and routinized
that artists and appreciative viewers turn to the arts for adventures of the spirit?

VISIBLE
IMAGE
AND
INVISIBLE
FAITH

hen the apostle Paul preached in Ephesus, he so angered the silversmiths of that city that he nearly lost his life. This incident recorded in the Acts of the Apostles is marvelously compact in describing Paul's encounter with rioting artisans whose livelihood was endangered by the apostle's preaching. The essence of Paul's message was that faith in Christ and the worship of God do not depend upon images made by human hands. Witnessing to the experience of the early Christians, and in light of his own Jewish background, Paul directly challenged a religious tradition in which images were indeed a necessary part of religious rites and a basic language for public communication.

Throughout the ancient Mediterranean world carved and painted images adorned temples and enhanced ritual observances, both public and private. Paul's travels in the Greco-Roman world brought him into contact with imagistic cultures completely antithetical to the Jewish environment in which he had been reared. The strictest rabbinic interpretation of the second commandment forbade not only the image of God but also the images of any living being.

This confrontation between Paul and the silversmiths is more than a record of one of the perilous events in his ministry, because it also illustrates radically different views about religion and its relationship to the visual arts. The crisis focuses attention upon a conflict over image use and religious experience, a conflict that has reverberated through the centuries. And Paul's preaching has provided fundamental arguments for those like-minded Christians who find no place for images in religious ritual or devotional practice.

Today we may find the violence of the silversmiths hard to understand, for our contemporary view of art is so far removed

Visible Image and Invisible Faith

from the religious sphere that it is difficult for us to see what the commotion was all about. In today's world the artist has a special status, not unlike that of the seer and prophet in earlier times. Some envision a career in the arts as a search for liberation and truth—a way of making sense of life. In a culture dominated by mass media and technology, painters and sculptors are viewed as contemplative free spirits who have rejected the ordinary, confining work demanded by a highly routinized, computerized society. Such artists, especially those widely publicized by galleries and agents, bear little resemblance to the silversmiths in Ephesus who, seeing their livelihood threatened by the iconoclastic preaching of Paul, instigated a riot, threatening the life of the apostle.

In ancient Greco-Roman cities, artisans were not regarded as soul-searching visionaries, but gained recognition through their technical skill. Individual craftsmen appeared as distinct persons when objects were signed, yet the maker's signature on a work was a relatively late development. Stonecutters created images for public buildings that told stories about heroes, gods, and goddesses. Metalsmiths made objects for private devotion as well as for sacred sites and temples. Even in Roman times the sculptor was not an independent designer or executant of his craft; it is uncertain, for example, who designed and directed the work on Trajan's column. The sculptor worked as an imperial archivist, not as an "initiator of the composition, but a propagandist."[1] By contrast, our current opinion of contemporary artists more closely resemble Plato's attitude about the Greek

---

[1] Alison Burford, *Craftsmen in Greek and Roman Society* (Ithaca, NY: Cornell University Press, 1974), p. 13. Burford writes that signed pieces represented the craftsman's interest in taking responsibility for the technical and stylistic solutions accomplished in particular works. Such signed pieces were most common among sculptors and appeared in the seventh century B.C.E. In Athens, potters and painters began to sign their works in the second quarter of the sixth century. See pp. 212-217.

poets. In *Ion*, Socrates says that inspiration and possession, not knowledge, enable poets to write; they utter beautiful poems "not through their craft, but as persons possessed by some other power....These lovely poems are not of man or human workmanship, but are divine from the gods."[2]

Since the purpose of this book is to explore the role of images in the communication of religious meanings, it would be a useful beginning to look at the conflict at Ephesus in greater detail. That is, first we will consider briefly the tradition threatened by Paul's preaching. But this is not simply an academic exercise in looking backward; later we will see that many of the technological images in our own contemporary world function like images in the classical world. Statues and relief sculpture on ancient monuments communicated stories that identified Greeks and Romans, providing symbols of political and mythic authority. Similarly the popular arts today permeate public space, reinforcing the mythologies of a democratic society. We may speculate that a modern Paul who criticized some aspects of our own imagistic system might also be run out of town.

To understand the hostility that Paul's preaching evoked among image-makers in the late classical cultural centers, we need to consider the significance of rites and ceremonies, both public and private, and the roles that images played in them. There are important differences between ancient and modern concepts of religion, as the historian of religion Fustel de Coulanges has observed.

> The word *religion* did not signify what it signifies for
> us; by this word we understand a body of dogmas, a

---

[2] Plato, *The Collected Dialogues of Plato*, Edith Hamilton and Huntington Cairns, eds. (New York: Pantheon, 1961), p. 220.

Visible Image and Invisible Faith

> doctrine concerning God, a symbol of faith concern-
> ing what is in and around us. This same word among
> the ancients, signified rites, ceremonies, acts of exte-
> rior worship. The doctrine was of small account: the
> practices were the important part.[3]

The visual arts were intimately related to all early religions. Images and objects were necessary to both public and private acts of piety, while an autonomous, disconnected realm of art such as we have today simply did not exist. Instead of artists, there were painters, sculptors, potters, stone masons, and silver-smiths—all of whom pursued their crafts in a society where re-ligious, political, and aesthetic elements were fused. To il-lustrate this situation, let us consider some of the images and the roles they played in the classical tradition. I have chosen ex-amples from this tradition in part because of Paul's missionary activity among the Gentiles, but we will see later that the visual codes for the shaping of images in this culture were to make a profound impact on the mainstream of Christian art in the west.

In the classical Greek tradition, religious art and buildings—temples, treasuries, theaters and free-standing statuary—were clustered together in sacred precincts. This concentration at particular sites lasted well into Roman times. Each city had its sacred area where public and private acts of devotion were prac-ticed by the citizenry. The acropolis at Athens is perhaps the best known; other impressive sites were Olympia and Delphi. At these sites images functioned in three ways. First, they had a sacral role. The temple was considered to be the dwelling place of the deity, and a statue of a god or goddess was placed in the

---

[3] Fustel de Coulanges, *The Ancient City: A Study on the Religion, Laws, and Institutions of Greece and Rome* (Garden City, NY: Doubleday, 1955), p. 167.

cella or main room. Except for special festive ceremonies, the ordinary citizen viewed the personification of the god from the eastern portal of the temple. While some saw these images as embodiments of the deity, the more educated and sophisticated viewers regarded them as symbols.[4] Other kinds of images and objects served as votive offerings to gods and goddesses in gratitude for favors or as petitions. Second, these images also commemorated special persons, both living and dead, who distinguished themselves in battle, games, or political life. Finally, the painted and carved images that adorned the architecture at sacred sites performed a narrative, pedagogical function. The sculpture of temple pediments and friezes represented fundamental social myths that uneducated persons who could not read or write could still absorb visually. Through vase painting and relief sculpture, the Homeric accounts of the Hellenes and the action of gods and goddesses in human affairs reached the people.

Such arts rendered visible the events, myths, and deities that were particularly significant for the populace. These story-telling, figurative works brought to common people concrete embodiments of myth and a world view. More than merely descriptive, they also served a normative purpose in reminding ordinary people of values to emulate. There, before their eyes, were heroes, gods, and goddesses with whom they could identify. Judging by the expenditures of political leaders from Pericles to the Hellenistic monarchs, we can surmise that these rulers had some sense of the value of visual models to reinforce loyalty and strengthen ties to the body politic.

From the classical sculpture and the painting that has survived on Greek vases we can deduce what can be called a classi-

---

4 Edwyn Bevan, *Holy Images: An Inquiry into Idolatry and Image-Worship in Ancient Paganism and in Christianity* (London: George Allen & Unwin, 1940), pp. 21-30.

Visible Image and Invisible Faith

cal aesthetic, that is, a particular set of conventions or codes for transforming legends and myths into visual images. These formulae enable us to understand the process of communication that took place through the use of concrete, representational forms. The human figure was essential for visual narratives. While captions were often used, the viewer who was familiar with popular mythology could grasp the meaning visually through characteristic gestures, human actions, and symbols associated with heroes, gods, and goddesses. For example, the Greek goddess Athena, known as a warrior and protector of heroes, was usually portrayed with breastplate, helmet and spear, holding in her left hand a symbol of victory.

Next, the classical representation of the human figure depended on both careful observation and the process of abstracting or generalizing. There is ample evidence that the artists studied and analyzed the human figure with care and skill, yet classical Greek sculptors and painters, unlike the later Romans, stopped short of what we might call "realism." Their observations were balanced by a concern for a canon or an ideal. Finally, the classical artisans sought to create the illusion of space; they were interested in the interaction of figures and background. While scientific perspective was not worked out until the Renaissance, these earlier artists understood that overlapping shapes and diminishing scale could give the illusion of volume and three-dimensionality. Although the classical code was modified and transformed throughout the centuries, these fundamental principles of visual narrative have persisted throughout western culture.

Early Christian Rejection of Images

Wherever the apostles traveled in the Greco-Roman world they confronted cultures in which images were basic forms of public communication. To the Gentile, the second commandment was an absurdity; but to the apostles, as to their Jewish ancestors, the images of gods and heroes, votive sculptures, and mythologies in stone were idolatrous as well as irrelevant in a world governed by God. Moreover, Paul's preaching and missionary activity among the Gentiles came at a time when early Christians looked toward an imminent return of the Messiah and a radical transformation of the whole order of society. Paul's eschatological view of the world, as well as his emphasis upon faith alone, contributed to his devaluation of classical culture.

Even when messianic hopes dwindled, later church leaders had to cope with a hostile pagan environment in which images played a major role in communicating and perpetuating religious and political authority.

Some leaders of the early church both challenged pagan culture and encouraged a withdrawal from it. In H. Richard Niebuhr's important study, *Christ and Culture*, Tertullian is cited as representative of those figures in early Christianity who set Christ against culture. It was he who insisted on the authority of Christ in all spheres of human activity, and rejected a cultural witness to faith, especially in philosophy and the arts. This position, Niebuhr asserts, was the expression of the first relationship between Christ and culture—logically first, because it emphasizes the lordship of Christ as found in the New Testament, and chronologically first because it appears to be typical of the earliest Christians.[5]

The early church fathers were opposed both to the meanings expressed in the classical images and to the aesthetic forms themselves. Tertullian, for example, insisted that not only was the worship of an idol forbidden, but also the making of an idol by a Christian worker. In the early church, painters of idolatrous pictures were compared to harlots, drunkards, brothelkeepers,

---

5 H. Richard Niebuhr, *Christ and Culture* (New York: Harper & Row, 1956), p. 45.

Visible Image and Invisible Faith

and actors. Tertullian's views about images are very close to rabbinical attitudes, which forbade the making of a likeness of any kind. This stalwart iconoclast did not approve of the depiction of anything—sacred or secular; he believed that "for the servants of God the whole expanse of the universe is thus excluded for the purposes of such an art."[6]

The Alexandrine patristic theologians, Clement and Origen, also argued against the making of images. While these men assimilated the classical learning of Greece and transformed much of its philosophy for Christian theology, they rejected Greek culture's visual aesthetic. Clement refers to Moses, who "made an express and public law against the making of any carved or molten or moulded or painted image and representation, in order that we might not direct our attention to sensible objects, but might proceed to the intelligential." For Origen, pagan image worship drags the soul down instead of directing the mind to a divine invisible reality. Clement, echoing the Platonic view, also maintains that images are not "true." Human beings are images of God—but an image of the image, the statues made in the likeness of human beings and far removed from the truth, appear only as a "fleeting impression." He considered preoccupation with images as "madness in a life."[7]

Yet in spite of these denunciations, paintings began to appear in the ritual spaces of early Christianity. Scholars have speculated about the reason for the gap between the strictures against images and their growing importance in the church. While educated theologians assimilated and transformed the philosophical traditions of the classical world, the common people they

---

6 Bevan, p. 86.

7 *Ibid.*, pp. 107, 87.

sought to convert and instruct were accustomed to images, to *seeing* sacred stories.

Missionaries and apologists preaching and teaching the Christian gospel in the Mediterranean world came face to face with country and urban people who had learned their religious, social, and political views primarily from narrative images and objects. If the church wanted to appeal to these groups and communicate to them, it had to speak, at least in part, that common visual language. Some church leaders understood this. Paulinus, Bishop of Nola, recognized that in order to attract people to Christianity from pagan religions, images were important. He was one of the first leaders to justify such pictures as a means of instructing the unlearned in sacred stories. The crowds who came to St. Felix were, in his words, peasant people "not devoid of religion but not able to read"; they were converted to Christian faith through gazing at images of the works of the saints.[8] In contrast to Tertullian's earlier world-rejecting attitudes, Paulinus expressed a positive view of images and their uses in conversion and instruction.

Yet even before this, some Christians had begun to appropriate visual language in some ceremonial spaces, and in the environment of classical culture a Christian iconic aesthetic slowly emerged. By medieval times churches had over the centuries found a narrative role for the visual arts similar to that of the classical world. On their facades were carved the figures and stories of sacred history; inside there were images and objects—representations in glass, paint, wood, metal, and stone—which served as aids to devotion. Yet always present, ever ready to erupt, was a persistent aniconic attitude which resisted and

---

[8] R. C. Godschmidt, *Paulinus' Churches at Nola: Texts, Translations and Commentary* (Amsterdam: N. V. Noord-Hollandsche Uitgeuers Maatschappij, 1940), p. 63. See also Bevan, pp. 124-125.

Visible Image and Invisible Faith

often sought to reform such use of the image. Bernard of Clair-vaux expressed this in the twelfth century, while iconoclastic movements surfaced dramatically during the Protestant Refor-mation. Before looking at the manifestations of this conflict in the modern era, I want to highlight certain moments of the past which illustrate how religious concerns may evoke both an iconic and aniconic aesthetic.

Toward an Iconic Aesthetic

In the Roman catacombs and in the Christian baptistry at Dura-Europos, a garrison city on the Euphrates at the border of the ancient Roman empire, important instances of pre-Con-stantinian painting in ritual settings have been found. In the catacombs frescoes of the late second and third centuries embody the basic conventions of Roman painting, while at the same time significantly modifying its forms, functions and sym-bols. The paintings are located in areas that had special mean-ing to the individual and community. Christian burial was accompanied by the expectation of resurrection and Christ's re-turn, and at these burial sites the images celebrated victory over death and anticipated the world to come.

Clearly the primary concern of the Christian community was not technical proficiency in representation, but the expressive significance of the image. For example, there is no comparison between the beautifully crafted images in the Pompeiian Villa of Mysteries and the small, sketchy ones that appear in Roman catacombs. In this respect Christian paintings resemble those found in pagan and Jewish catacombs of the time. Art historian Ernst Kitzinger has called attention to the aesthetic revolution that occurred during the third century in which "classical art transformed itself." Christianity did not, he says, "spearhead" these new forms; but since it grew rapidly during this period, it appropriated the aesthetic.[9]

From the reservoir of this late classical style Christian artisans drew the fundamental language of the human figure, its gestures, expressions, and actions in space. However crude the drawing or painting, Christian faith and hope could be "told" through figural representations. Moreover, the apparent lack of technical skill or concern for style contributed to the animated, expressionistic rendering of the human figure that suggested soul or spirit. This was a symbolic asset for Christians primarily concerned with the non-material and transcendent dimensions of human experience.

Some paintings in the catacombs seem to be portraits of the deceased, while others illustrate biblical motifs. Popular subjects included the Three Hebrews in the Fiery Furnace, the Sacrifice of Abraham, and the Good Shepherd. Most scholars agree that deliverance through God's action is a major theme expressed in both Old and New Testament symbols. In the catacomb of Priscilla, the three Hebrew youths, dressed in Turkish costume, have their arms upraised in a gesture of supplication. Above them is an image of a dove which suggests divine intervention—the angel of the Lord who came down to the furnace. Similarly the depiction of Abraham and Isaac shows faith put to the ultimate test. Numerous Old Testament stories served as prototypes pointing to the early Christian experience of salvation. Some of the portrayals are cryptic—the eucharist, for example, was frequently symbolized in a small vignette of loaves

---

9   Ernst Kitzinger, *Byzantine Art in the Making: Main Lines of Stylistic Development in Mediterranean Art, 3rd-7th Century* (Cambridge, MA: Harvard University Press, 1980), pp. 19-20. See also: Kurt Weitzmann, ed., *Age of Spirituality: A Symposium* (New York: The Metropolitan Museum of Art, published in association with Princeton University Press, 1980) and H. P. L'Orange, *Art Forms and Civic Life in the Late Roman Empire* (Princeton: Princeton University Press, 1965).

Visible Image and Invisible Faith

and fish—while other signs were conventional. The fish became a popular one, deriving its significance from an acrostic based on the initial Greek letters of the words "Jesus Christ, Son of God, Savior."

Since the catacombs were not places of public worship, their images suggest an unusual attempt to express faith. Art historians have contrasted the sepulchral representations of the catacombs to traditional didactic religious art, interpreting images of exhortation and encouragement. They can also be viewed as a confessional art. Against the background of Christian hope for deliverance and confidence in resurrection, the images are like prayers, which have both a private and a public dimension. This experimental aspect, particularly prominent in the extreme situation of persecution, appropriates the late classical aesthetic to communicate an intensity and pathos which later disappears.[10] With the conversion of Constantine the relationship between faith and image changed, and after the early fifth century, the catacombs were only infrequently used for burial.

A different kind of religious painting was discovered early in the twentieth century. At Dura-Europos excavations uncovered the remains of many kinds of religious sanctuaries, including a Jewish synagogue and a Christian baptistry. A garrison city at the outer edges of the Roman empire, Dura-Europos was a multi-cultural crossroads and caravan city inhabited by people of diverse religious traditions. After it was attacked and destroyed about the middle of the third century C.E., desert sand covered the ruins of the city until its accidental discovery.

Paintings from both the Jewish synagogue and the Christian baptistry at Dura-Europos have provided extraordinary material for scholars who previously had only fragments to work with.

---

[10] *Ibid.*, p. 21.

The findings at the synagogue suggest that the narrow interpretation of the second commandment was not always strictly followed by Jewish communities. The interior walls of the House of Assembly are painted with horizontal bands of scenes from biblical history and lives of heroes such as Moses, Elijah, Abraham and Ezekiel. Joseph Gutmann, a specialist in Jewish art, suggests that the key to the cycle of paintings in the synagogue lies in understanding the prevailing Judaism of that period. He contends that Dura belongs to a radically new type of Judaism out of which Christianity grew and was nourished. It substituted prayers within the synagogues for practices at the Temple and elevated the scholar-rabbi, doing away with priestly intermediaries. Moreover, it offered eternal life through personal salvation of the soul and bodily resurrection. Gutmann speculates that, seen in light of this new form of Judaism, the paintings reflect its theological teachings and liturgy. Thus the cycle of paintings can be analyzed on two levels. First, the architectural and artistic significance may be studied; second, the images and space may be examined in relation to the "now lost, invisible, active liturgical function"—the ceremonies and prayers that enlivened the place of worship.[11]

Although there were abundant wall paintings in the major worship area of the synagogue, in the corresponding area of the Christian building, the Assembly Hall, there were none. However, images found in the Christian baptistry have offered scholars new perspectives on the origins of Christian art. Understanding these paintings is a complex task; like all images, those of the early Christian baptistry are subject to a variety of interpretations. According to Erwin Panofsky the most elemen-

---

[11] Joseph Gutmann, ed., *The Dura-Europos Synagogue: A Re-evaluation (1932-1972)*, (American Academy of Religion, Society of Biblical Literature, 1973), pp. 144-146. See also Karl H. Kraeling, *The Synagogue* (New Haven: Yale University Press, 1956).

Visible Image and Invisible Faith

tary level of symbolism, the *primary* one, depends upon our reservoir of sense experiences and perceptions. We refer unfamil-
iar images to what we already know. At this primary level we
identify marks that signify a man, a woman, and commonly experienced objects and environments such as mountains, trees,
sun, moon, or horizon. After that we move to a *secondary* level,
where recognition comes only after mythic, ritual or cultural in-
doctrination has taken place. Two stick figures of a man and a
woman, a tree, and a serpent portray Adam and Eve and the
Fall for viewers familiar with the Bible. But even here we need
to be cautious, for we cannot be sure that our present understanding of certain biblical stories and symbols is the same as
that of the early Christians.

In his study of the baptistry, Karl Kraeling, one of the Yale
scholars associated with the Dura excavations, has proposed
three principles to help our understanding of its images. First,
interpretation should be in keeping with the general historical
and cultural context to which the decorations belong. This context should be understood to include the pictorial decorations
and pagan temples and the Jewish synagogue at Dura. Second,
any interpretation should keep in mind the purpose which the
baptistry served, that of solemnizing the baptismal rite. Third, it
should develop as far as possible out of those Christian sources
that are most clearly related to the region from which the decorations come and to the purpose which they serve.[12] Kraeling
has also emphasized the close relations between the paintings
and contemporary liturgy, analyzing the images of the baptistry
in light of the liturgical and literary sources that were available
to the small Christian community in the mid-third century. He

---

[12] Karl H. Kraeling, *The Christian Building* (New Haven: Dura-Europos Publications, 1967), pp. 178, 179. See also: M. Rostovtzeff, *Dura-Europos and Its Art* (Oxford: The Clarendon Press, 1938).

has found the selection of images and their organization on the walls are particularly suited to the rite of baptism which took place there.

First and most important is the baptismal font on the west wall. Within an arched niche of the bapistry is a curved shape with a painted image of the Good Shepherd watching over his sheep and carrying a large one on his shoulders. In the lower left-hand part of this area is a crude sketch, almost graffiti-like, representing Adam and Eve with a tree and a serpent. Although the room is small, on the other walls are several painted vignettes. These include Christ's healing of the paralytic, who literally takes up his bed and walks; Christ walking on the water, reaching out to a sinking Peter as other disciples watch from a boat; the women at the well; and David and Goliath. A large, fragmented set of paintings related to the resurrection story covers the east and north walls. Taken together, all of these images emphasize the theme of salvation through the work and person of the savior, Jesus Christ. To these early Christians victory over sin and death was associated with the rite of baptism. Like the images found in the synagogue, these were related to the liturgy and derived from the baptismal practices and doctrines familiar to the local congregation.

Thus, in spite of the rejection of imgages by early church fathers, Christians did use them in their ritual spaces. However, the catacombs and the baptistry at Dura-Europos reveal only a very modest appropriation by Christians of the rich formal language of classical art. It was not until the Constantinian era that the visual arts began a dramatic development. Under the political leaders of the Holy Roman Empire, church building and decoration accelerated. The church of San Apollinare Nuovo in Ravenna was built between 494 and 526 during the reign of the Arian ruler, Theodoric. When the city later came under the domination of the Emperor Justinian, some changes in the

Visible Image and Invisible Faith

church's interior were made, and the building was reconsecrated by orthodox Catholics.

The interior wall surfaces above the columns of the nave are covered with three levels of shimmering mosaics. On the left wall, at the lowest level, are figures of female martyrs processing toward Mary, who is seated on a throne and holding the Christ child. To the right, on the south wall, is a parallel procession of male martyrs moving toward Christ. These processional figures replaced earlier mosaics which depicted King Theodoric and members of his court. On a second, higher level are single, majestic figures of Old and New Testament heroes which fill the space between the clerestory windows; above these are panels depicting sacred stories from the gospels. Mosaics on the north side describe episodes from the teaching and ministry of Christ, such as the raising of Lazarus and the healing of the paralytic and the man possessed by demons. Opposite, on the uppermost level of the south wall of the nave, a symbolic sequence moving from the altar toward the western entrance tells the story of Christ's passion, his death, and resurrection.

Such scenes are to be understood not only as visual narratives, but as representations of the liturgical drama: "the Savior's life, death, and resurrection did not happen once in the dim past...but take place mystically within the faithful themselves as they are enacted in the liturgy."[13] The biblical subjects at San Apollinare Nuovo, like those of the Dura Baptistry, appear to be selected and arranged to reinforce the liturgical rites that occur in the sacred space. At the same time, it needs to be noted, as Kitzinger has done, that originally the prime space, the lowest level, was filled with mosaic images of the Ostrogoth

---

[13] Otto Georg von Simson, *Sacred Fortress: Byzantine Art and Statecraft in Ravenna* (Chicago: University of Chicago Press, 1948), p. 79.

king and his retinue which ended up before the representations of Christ and the Virgin.[14]

By the late sixth century, images were found in churches thoughout Christendom, but certain dangers accompanied their widespread acceptance. Gregory the Great sanctioned the narrative role of images, yet made a fundamental distinction between worshiping an image and learning from it. Responding to a bishop from Marseilles, who had broken up pictures in his church to prevent his congregation from offering homage to them, Gregory concluded that the bishop was right to forbid the worship of images but wrong to destroy them:

> It is one thing to offer homage to (*adorare*) a picture and quite another thing to learn, by way of a story told in a picture, to what homage ought to be offered.... If anyone desires to make images, do not forbid him; only prohibit by all the means in your power the worshipping of images.[15]

Gregory's distinction between learning from images and paying homage to them restored and institutionalized one of the principal functions of classical visual images—the story-telling or narrative role. At the same time, he was clear about their misuse. His attitude reflected and shaped the subsequent use of images in western Christendom. Throughout Europe, Christian motifs and symbols appeared in churches, baptistries, and sepulchres. Liturgical objects, reliquaries, and sarcophagi were embellished with images, and manuscripts were handsomely il-

---

[14] Kitzinger, *Byzantine Art*, pp. 62-64.

[15] Bevan, *Holy Images*, p. 126. In the eastern church the use of of images is complex; icons are not simply representations, but "manifestations of the heavenly archetypes." See ch. 1 in Ernst Benz, *The Eastern Orthodox Church* (New York: Anchor, 1963) and Leonid Ouspensky and Vladimir Lossky, *The Meaning of Icons* (Crestwood, NY: St. Vladimir's, 1983).

Visible Image and Invisible Faith

luminated with pictures illustrating the sacred stories of Scripture.

The examples used thus far reflect ways in which image usage by Christians drew upon the transformations of Greco-Roman forms set in motion during the third century. Over time these changing pictorial conventions were used to communicate Christian symbols and enliven liturgical spaces. The use of elaborate media, such as mosaics, depended upon the patronage and support of powerful political and religious leaders. Yet those who supported the uses of images in Christian devotion, both public and private, were not preoccupied with what we think of today as art. When paintings and sculptures appeared in churches, they complemented the liturgy and were seen as aids to devotion or acts of piety. Even so, some theologians continued to be uneasy about images in worship spaces.

In the twelfth century appeared two Christian thinkers who responded to the visual arts in opposite ways. Suger, the Abbot of St. Denis, was a spokesman for the importance of the arts in the expression and evocation of faith. His work and writing affirmed the visual arts in worship. Suger's contemporary, Bernard of Clairvaux, on the other hand, is known for his criticism of images and his reforming vigor in bringing aesthetic simplicity to the buildings of the Cistercian order. Nevertheless, in Cistercian architecture there are important visual elements, and even in the total absence of images the buildings present an aesthetic of their own.

Both Suger and Bernard were symbolists, yet their activities and attitudes resulted in contradictory kinds of Christian aesthetics. They differ most notably on the use of figural art in the embellishment of liturgical space. Suger's aesthetic illuminates the philosophy of the *via affirmativa*. Material objects, whether natural or made by human hands, can inspire devotion, enhance meditation, and lead the soul to the experience of transcendence. Bernard's emphasis upon asceticism and his concern for

24

the primacy of the word in religious communication, however, led to a renunciation of visual images, particularly for monastics. Bernard's thought provides the basis for a *via negativa* in the visual arts, a rejection of images in pursuit of spirituality. This attitude, detected in some ancient and medieval thinkers, would surface again in twentieth-century artists in search of transcendent reality.

Suger was influential as a medieval advocate for the use of the arts in communicating and celebrating the gospel. His own account of the reconstruction and redecoration of the Abbey of St. Denis, an account which has been translated and interpreted by Erwin Panofsky, described materials, construction problems, and ideas on ornamentation. The abbot documented the struggles and joy he experienced in the redecoration of the famous French abbey church. For him the architecture, stained glass, and liturgical objects were orchestrated into a great canticle of praise.

Panofsky attributes Suger's religious aesthetic to his interest in the ideas of Pseudo-Dionysius the Areopagite. A mixture of neo-Platonic and Christian doctrines, these ideas described the fluid, vital connections between the highest spiritual sphere and the material world. Since all visible things are "material lights" that mirror the ultimate Light, the contemplation of objects can lead to the source of all goodness and being. In appropriating the mysticism of the *via affirmativa*, one could apply it to all natural objects and artifacts.

> This stone or that piece of wood is a light to me....
> As I perceive such and similar things...they
> enlighten me...and soon, under the guidance of rea-
> son I am led through all things to that cause of all

Visible Image and Invisible Faith

> things which endows them with place and order, with number, species and kind, with goodness and beauty and essence, and with all other grants and gifts.[16]

Yet recent scholars think that Panofsky placed undue emphasis upon Suger's familiarity with Pseudo-Dionysius and, indeed, upon the abbot's role in architectural innovations at St. Denis.[17] At the same time, Suger's writings indicate that he personally appreciated the work of craftsmen in wood, stone, metal, and precious gems. For him the liturgical objects and spaces fashioned by artisans offered a special opportunity for self-transcendence:

> Thus when—out of my delight in the beauty of the house of God—the loveliness of the many-colored gems has called me away from external cares, and worthy meditation has induced me to reflect, transferring that which is material to that which is immaterial...then it seems to me that I see myself dwelling, as it were, in some strange region of the universe which neither exists entirely in the slime of the earth nor entirely in the purity of Heaven; and that, by the grace of God, I can be transported from this inferior to that higher world....[18]

Recent interpreters of Suger argue that this passage indicates how he found the arts conducive to religious contemplation, grounded in the physical beauty of the building. "Religious ar-

---

[16] Erwin Panofsky, *Abbot Suger On the Abbey Church of St. Denis and its Art Treasures* (Princeton: Princeton University Press, 1979), p. 20.

[17] Peter Kidson, "Panofsky, Suger and St. Denis," *Journal of the Warburg and Courtland Institutes* (1987 1:5,6. Peter Kidson contends that the light-metaphysic of Suger has been overestimated. There is no evidence, he says, that Suger had empathy with or an understanding of the neo-Platonic aspect of Christian theology.

[18] Panofsky, *Suger*, pp. 63,65.

chitecture was here performing what sensitive and imaginative souls might consider to be its proper function, namely offering a foretaste of paradise through the senses...it brings heaven down to earth."[19] Suger himself noted in a later passage that the liturgical images and objects are not in themselves salvific. It is the eucharist that is essential, and he agreed with his more ascetic critics that "a saintly mind, a pure heart, a faithful intention" are central to religious devotion. But he insisted that devotion expressed through beautifully crafted objects was appropriate.

While the abbot's efforts focused on the redecoration of St. Denis near Paris, other twelfth-century churches exemplify the increasing presence of images for instruction and contemplation. St. Mary Madeleine in Vézelay, central France, is one of the best preserved of the Romanesque pilgrimage churches. Although it was damaged by fire as well as by iconoclasts of the French Enlightenment, one can still find there rich and beautiful examples of Romanesque architecture. It allowed for the circulation of the pilgrims throughout the sanctuary, in the aisles, around the ambulatory and down steps into the crypt beneath the altar, which once housed relics associated with the patron saint. A modern pilgrim can still move in and out of its spaces, following the narratives that twelfth-century stone carvers created out of biblical stories, moral allegories, and the virtues and vices.

At the entry to the sanctuary are three portals whose complex iconography has fascinated art historians.[20] While the precise meaning has been debated, their general theological sym-

---

[19] Kidson, p. 7.

[20] Emile Male interpreted the symbolism of the central portal as the descent of the Holy Spirit. Adolf Katzenellenbogen believes that the iconography is more complex and that different events—the ascension and the descent of the Holy Spirit—are combined. See his "The Central Tympanum at Vézelay" in *The Art Bulletin* 26:3:141-151.

Visible Image and Invisible Faith

bolism is clear: these portals through which worshipers pass into the ritual space of the sanctuary dramatize the Incarnation. Over the south portal the tympanum depicts the birth of Christ, the moment when "the Word became flesh and dwelt among us," the human beginning of the mystery of the Incarnation. Above the north portal the sculpture on the tympanum portrays the appearance of Christ to his disciples on the road to Emmaus and his ascension into heaven. The large central portal is generally assumed to represent Pentecost: the manifestation of the Holy Spirit to the followers of Jesus and the beginnings of the church.

While interpretations of some details of these portals may differ, it seems clear that these gateways to the liturgy and sacraments depict the essential message of Christian faith. God assumed the form of a human being and dwelt among us; after Christ's resurrection he appeared to his disciples and commissioned them to go thoughout the world to teach and preach; and the Holy Spirit came to them to manifest his living and continuing presence. Missing in these portals is the story of the crucifixion, death, and resurrection, for that part of the Christian drama takes place within the sanctuary, in the liturgy itself.

The central portal is especially compelling in the way that it involves us in complex dimensions of time and space. In the innermost part of the tympanum we see the appearance of the Holy Spirit, an event that reverberates throughout human time and space. On the outer sections, a sculptural succession of human events radiates outward from Pentecost. On the lintel is depicted a spectrum of diverse physical and ethnic types, the world of humanity to whom the gospel was addressed. Perhaps the most poignant images in this central portal are those showing the continuing presence of the Holy Spirit in the everyday world of the twelfth century. In the outermost parts of the semicircle is portrayed the yearly cycle—the signs of the zodiac and the labors associated with each season. These motifs can be seen in many Romanesque and Gothic churches, but here they are drawn into the pentecostal drama and the movement of the Holy Spirit throughout human history. The seasonal cycle begins with a peasant cutting bread, and the year ends with a parallel eucharistic symbol, a man taking wine from a cup. In between, circulating around the arch, are images of the seasons and the activities that measure human time and experience. One especially sympathetic image occurs toward the end of the yearly cycle. Within a small circular frame is a tired old man, carrying on his shoulders a smaller elderly woman—a poignant image of human frailty and pathos, marking the limits of our claim on time and season.

Upon entering the sanctuary, one encounters an abundance of sculptures which crown the columns attached to vertical pillars. Looking closely at the carved capitals, one can see that often several related events are depicted in sequence. Each facet portrays an episode and, encountering these facets, one follows a continuous visual narration. For example, one capital details the story of the evil rich man and the beggar Lazarus. In the center portion the rich man is shown on his death bed as demons grab his soul, which is personified as a small figure emerging from his mouth. One side of the capital shows the soul of Lazarus transported to heaven by angelic figures; the other represents him resting in the bosom of Abraham. Other capitals use allegorical themes, such as Paul and the Mill of Christ. Still others illustrate virtues and vices. It takes little more than a brief look at these works to appreciate their appeal both to the uneducated and to the theologically sophisticated in expressing and nurturing Christian faith.

As pilgrims circulated down the aisles, around the apse and to the crypt below, each capital presented a story to be read. Moving through the spaces, they absorbed biblical history and religious allegories through visual symbols. And before leaving

Visible Image and Invisible Faith

the space of the sanctuary, worshipers were drawn into the great drama itself by their participation in the eucharist.

Yet to some religious leaders the images at Vézelay and other churches were tolerated primarily as a means to instruct the illiterate. For persons deeply committed to the religious life no such aids to devotion were necessary. Indeed for those called to the monastic life, images were considered a distraction and, worse, a shameful extravagance.

Bernard of Clairvaux: The Aniconic Aesthetic

The opinions of Suger's contemporary, Bernard of Clairvaux, who objected to the use of images and objects in the church and sought to eliminate them, were expressed in a famous letter to William, Abbot of St. Thierry. He writes critically of the "usual" custom of images in churches, describing them as "curious carvings and paintings which attract the worshiper's gaze and hinder his attention."[21] But, he adds, let this comment pass if bishops, responsible for both the "wise and unwise," are unable to arouse the devotion of worldly people by spiritual things and try then to do so by material adornment. While Bernard is willing to tolerate images under certain circumstances, he completely opposes them in monastic churches. Bishops may have an excuse for permitting images as a means to devotion; monks do not.

> But we who have now come forth from the people; we who have left all the precious and beautiful things of the world for Christ's sake....Whose devotion, pray, do we monks intend to excite by things?[22]

---

[21] Elizabeth Gilmore Holt, ed., A Documentary History of Art, vol 1, The Middle Ages and the Renaissance (Garden City, NY: Doubleday, 1957), p. 19.

[22] Ibid., p. 20.

In the course of his letter, Bernard develops a number of objections. One passage shows very clearly his preference for "the word" as he offers what has become a recurring argument:

> In short, so many and so marvelous are the varieties of divers shapes on every hand, that we are more tempted to read in the marble than in our books, and to spend the whole day wondering at these things, rather than in meditating on the law of God.[23]

For Bernard, worship and contemplation were centered on the word of God. He would have had little sympathy for Suger's position that images can initiate and inspire reflections on God's glory in ways that words cannot. At most, he would have admitted validity of the image only for the uneducated.

Bernard reinforced his position by pointing to the exploitation and abuse of images. In the same letter to William he observes that in the presence of material splendor, persons are more "kindled to offer gifts than to pray."

> Their eyes are feasted with relics cased in gold, and their purse-strings are loosed. They are shown a most comely image of some saint, whom they think all the more saintly that he is the more gaudily painted. Men run to kiss him, and are invited to give; there is more admiration for his comeliness than veneration for his sanctity.[24]

Elsewhere, Bernard showed an appreciation of images and a sensitivity to a different kind of offense: their desecration and

---

[23] *Ibid.*, p. 21.

[24] *Ibid.*, p. 20.

Visible Image and Invisible Faith

defilement. He notes that where pictures of saints are inlaid on floors, insensitive persons spit on an angel's face and the "countenance of some saint is ground under the heel of a passer-by."[25]

Finally, Bernard's arguments gather ethical force and intensity in a condemnation that reminds one of the wrath of the prophet Amos when he lashed out at those who sold the righteous for silver. "The church," Bernard writes, "is resplendent in her walls, beggarly in her poor." Churches adorned with glistening, wonderfully fashioned precious objects feed the eye of the rich at the expense of the indigent. Stones are clothed in gold while human beings go naked. And while some people find delight in images, the needy find no relief. Bernard concludes with indignation, raising the question of the church's priorities and responsibilities: "For God's sake, if men are not ashamed of these follies, why at least do they not shrink from the expense?" He was convinced that the arts were an unnecessary luxury and that Christians ought first of all to be concerned for the poor.[26]

While Bernard was critical of the visual arts, he assiduously cultivated the arts of writing and preaching. For him the word was paramount in religious communication. Etienne Gilson has written that the Cistercian leader, schooled in the tradition of Cicero and Augustine, took great pains with writing. Bernard's walls were bare, but his literary style was not. "In spite of all his formidible asceticism St. Bernard was no puritan when it came

---

[25] *Ibid.*, pp. 20, 21. See also Meyer Schapiro, "On the Aesthetic Attitude in Romanesque Art," *Romanesque Art: Selected Papers* (New York: George Braziller, 1977) pp. 6-10.

[26] *Ibid.*

to literature."[27] In another context he described the monk's special literary talents:

> St. Bernard, indeed, achieved a highly personal Latin style, adorned but not overcharged with Biblical citations, harmonious, and of a deeply intimate sonority...at once faithful to the classical tradition and rejoicing in the liberty of a native tongue.[28]

Gilson related these literary gifts to Bernard's deliberation in his earlier years about becoming a "man of letters." The historian concluded that as a monk the Abbot of Clairvaux pursued both the art of writing and a commitment to the mystical life.

Bernard was one of the most powerful and influential churchmen in twelfth-century Europe; nevertheless, despite his critique, the appetite for images of devotion and instruction increased. In the next century the visual language of the "gospel in stone" would reach unprecedented splendor and complexity in Gothic art and architecture.[29] Yet Bernard's emphasis upon the nourishment of faith by preaching and Scripture had a profound effect upon church building, where his influence led to the development of a different kind of aesthetic—a religious symbolism that was aniconic, that is, devoid of representational imagery.

---

[27] Etienne Gilson, *The Mystical Theology of Saint Bernard*, trans. A. H. C. Downes (New York: Sheed & Ward, 1940), p. 63.

[28] *Ibid.*, p. 7.

[29] Ernst Kitzinger, *Early Medieval Art in the British Museum* (London: The Trustees of the British Museum, 1963), pp. 81, 82. Kitzinger has pointed out that the plain assembly-room of early Christians gradually became a "new and complicated architectural organism....It becomes a kind of fugue, an architectural hymn, a manifestation of the glory of God." The medieval cathedral proclaimed concretely and visibly the dogma of the church.

Visible Image and Invisible Faith

The Cistercian order was formed in 1098 at Citeaux by a group of Benedictine monks who sought a stricter observance of the Rule of St. Benedict, a return to simplicity and manual labor and a renewed emphasis upon withdrawal from the world. In 1112, Bernard, at the age of twenty-two, joined this order along with thirty devoted followers—brothers, relations, and friends. Three years later Bernard and a small group of monks were sent to found a colony in Champagne, in a wild, undomesticated valley called Wormwood, where they built a monastery which he named Clairvaux. From these humble beginnings—a wooden structure which housed chapel, dormitory, and refectory under one roof—would emerge one of the most powerful cultural forces of the twelfth century. Reflecting Bernard's zeal and energy, the order grew rapidly and spread thoughout Europe and into England. In Bernard's lifetime alone, over a hundred and fifty Cistercian monasteries were established.

Cistercians tended to seek forbidding, out-of-the-way places in which to establish their monasteries. Cultivating and developing undesirable or difficult terrain, they became unusually skilled in the practical arts and sciences. They invented techniques which turned swamps into arable land and barren places into gardens. They excelled in agriculture and animal husbandry and discovered new, unique ways to market farm produce and livestock. Their practical, innovative work left a deep imprint on the culture of Europe.

Like other monastic groups, the Cistercians constructed their monasteries as complex, self-sufficient functional units. In view of Bernard's position on the use of painting, sculpture, and ornament, one might conclude that the power of visual forms would be negligible in churches built under his influence. But a particular type of beauty resulted from this rejection of images and the creation of fitting places for liturgy and contemplation. Out of their concern to develop simple, imageless spaces came certain visual elements and principles which constitute a distinctive aniconic aesthetic.

In his letter to William of St. Thierry, Bernard criticized not only paintings and carvings but also the "immoderate length" and "superfluous breadth" of church design. Simplicity of forms and scale became a characteristic feature of Cistercian churches. Their basic plan was in the shape of a cross. While this type of plan had been used throughout the history of church building in the west, the Cistercians clarified and simplified the spaces and developed a more modest scale for the height and breadth of the building. The extension of the eastern end of the church, for example, was reduced in size and often squared off in contrast to the more elaborate forms of the apse that were developing in other Romanesque churches.

Bernard's influence can be most clearly seen in the instructions that were circulated in the order. These instructions were part of a code of laws developed to ensure unanimity and conformity of monastic discipline. Scholars ascertain that two important statutes were legislated between 1115 and 1119.[30] Statute 10 regulated the materials and forms of liturgical art.

> 10. *What is permissible or non permissible for us to have of gold, silver, jewels, and silk:* Altar cloths and the garments of those ministering are to be without silk except the stole and maniple. No chasuble is to be had, unless of one color. All ornaments, vessels, and utensils of the monastery are to be without gold, silver, or jewels except the chalice and the fistula, which two alone we are allowed to have when of silver and gilded, but by no means when golden.[31]

---

[30] Conrad Rudolph, "The 'Principal Founders' and the Early Artistic Legislation at Citeaux," *Studies in Cistercian Art and Architecture* (Kalamazoo, MI: Cistercian Publications, 1987) 3:29.

[31] *Ibid.*, p. 4.

Visible Image and Invisible Faith

Statute 20 prohibited monumental painting and sculpture:

> 20. *Concerning sculptures, paintings, and the wooden cross:* We forbid sculptures or paintings in either our churches or in any of the rooms of the monastery, because when attention is turned to such things the advantage of good meditation or the discipline of religious gravity is often neglected. However, we do have painted crosses which are of wood.[32]

Cistercian scholar Conrad Rudolph points out that the elimination of paintings and sculpture is designated as a restriction to the monk alone. Gregory the Great had already presented the authoritative position on imagery in the western church, justifying it as a means of instructing those unable to read for themselves. Thus the Cistercian strictures were addressed to "literati," the monastic communities. Rudolph points out, however, that this prohibition of excessive art affected the social involvement of the monasteries. It meant, for example, the termination of the practice "by the duke or any other secular power, of holding court at Citeaux, something which up until that time had been the custom there." These strictures also had an effect upon the lucrative aspects of pilgrimages; there were no forms in the monastic churches to instruct the illiterate, the pilgrims.[33] Within these restrictions, or perhaps because of them, Cistercian builders developed forms which are notable for an austere, abstract beauty. The church at Fontenay, built between 1139 and 1147 in western France, is one of their better preserved buildings.

Looking at the facade of the church, one is impressed first by its simplicity. A single portal marks the entry into the nave, a rectangular doorway framed by angled recessions and a single

---

[32] *Ibid.*, p. 6.

[33] *Ibid.*, pp. 8, 16, 17.

column on each side. The semi-circular area over the door, in contrast to the tympana at Vézelay, has no images. Above the portal are levels of windows which provide a horizontal geometric pattern for the upper part of the facade. All of these abstract shapes are drawn together by a long, thin, continuous horizontal band that projects slightly from the wall. There are no towers to interrupt the simplicity of the facade at Fontenay, since they were forbidden in the early days of the order.

Within the church is a radiance of light that illuminates austere architectural forms: unadorned capitals, cruciform pillars, arched spaces leading toward the altar. The light from the east windows above the altar dominates the interior space. Abstract shapes—circles, squares, rectangles, ellipses—are both ornamental and structural. In effect, the functional forms, luminous in their simplicity, become the language of ornament. Light upon simple surfaces, patterns of repeated geometric shapes, the compelling vertical and horizontal rhythms of support and buttresses—all, despite the lack of images, create an aesthetic vocabulary.

Elements of an Aniconic Aesthetic

As they clarified liturgical space in their sanctuaries, Cistercian builders fused abstract shapes and functional forms into a new symbolic and ornamental order. In contrast to the sculptured images at Vézelay, they developed aniconic, or imageless, metaphors and symbols. But the builders were not self-consciously preoccupied with aesthetics; Bernard and the Cistercians were, first and foremost, reformers of the monastic life. Historians have commented upon Bernard's indifference to the beauty of the visible world and artful objects. Yet the rigorous simplicity and search for the most fitting context for prayer and worship led the Cistercian builders, knowingly or unknowingly, to an alternative aesthetic with its own inherent beauty and potential symbolism.

Visible Image and Invisible Faith

A primary visual element in these churches—light—has its own symbolic associations with divine reality. We have seen that Suger understood the symbolism of light. Indeed, the use of this powerful aesthetic phenomenon is found in the art and architecture of many cultures, including the religions of antiquity. Edwyn Bevan, a scholar concerned with cross-cultural religious symbols, in his book *Symbolism and Belief,* relates some of its properties to its pervasive use as a religious symbol. Light reveals itself at the same time that it reveals other things. Moreover, a luminous body—the sun, for example, which sends forth light continuously—seems to suffer no loss of substance. Bevan points out further the traditional association of light with truth, joy, awe, and glory.[34]

In Cistercian churches light has its own special qualities. The windows are channels for clear rays which penetrate into and illuminate the sanctuary. Stained glass, in contrast, produces a deeper luminosity which softens stone pillars and shrouds structural elements with mysterious color. Whereas figural, colored patterns brighten and darken with the movement of the sun, often dazzling the eyes with kaleidoscopic changes, the light in the Cistercian sanctuaries sharpens rather than diffuses. It reveals the lines and masses of the sparse, clean forms of the interior. Changes in intensity, of course, reflect the hours and seasons, but the exclusion of color emphasizes the dramatic patterns of light and darkness shaped by abstract architectural forms.

Both aesthetically and symbolically, the dominant feature of Cistercian light is its revelatory quality. On the one hand, bright clear light reveals human and inanimate forms in all their starkness, neither embellished nor clothed by color. This disclo-

---

[34] Edwyn Bevan, *Symbolism and Belief* (Boston: Beacon Press, 1957), pp. 125-150.

sure is congenial to the Cistercian emphasis upon humility and purity and their quest for simplicity. But light itself becomes a symbol of divine, ineffable reality—the source of being as well as of seeing. Its clarity and brilliance may easily become a visual affirmation of the mystical poetry expressed by the psalmist: "In thy light do we see light."

A second formal and symbolic element in the Cistercian aniconic aesthetic is the use of abstract shapes—circles, half-circles, squares, and ellipses—which orchestrate a variety of spaces. Similar forms were of course used in other Romanesque buildings, but the shapes, as in semi-circular tympana, were usually adorned with sculpture. In Cistercian buildings the unembellished construction reveals a beauty of its own. The absence of ornament clarifies the elegance of line and mass. From repeated patterns of such forms comes a different kind of ornamental and symbolic vocabulary.

In contrast to the narrative sculpture at St. Mary Madeleine, no stories are being told. Yet the simplicity and purity of the primary geometric shapes generate symbolic overtones. One may deduce a kind of "meaning" from the deliberate elimination of representational imagery and from the resolve to use only pure forms as ornament. These decisions can be linked to a larger, more ancient mystical tradition in which numbers, abstract forms and relationships symbolize religious knowledge and experience; knowingly or not, Cistercian builders were constructing a similar aniconic aesthetic in which visual experience itself undergoes a purification. Materials are purged of concrete references to familiar human experience. Through the intensification and amplification of pure geometric forms one is drawn into an environment that empties the mind of all images and prepares it for ritual.

A third element in the Cistercian aesthetic is the concern for order and proportionality. Peter Berger in *A Rumor of Angels* refers to "signals of transcendence," experiences that point beyond

Visible Image and Invisible Faith

natural or human reality. The first of these signals is the human propensity for order.

> Throughout most of human history human beings have believed that the created order of society, in one way or another, corresponds to an underlying order of the universe, a divine order that supports and justifies all human attempts at ordering.[35]

This desire for order, he says, is grounded in faith or trust in the ultimate order of the universe. The search for order is metaphysical, rather than ethical, and gives cosmic scope to the human need for meaning. What we may regard as a "signal of transcendence" in our contemporary secular world was, in the medieval world, a profound certainty. In some manuscripts we find the creator God literally portrayed as architect, using a compass to circumscribe and order the universe. This visual metaphor of divine order is a common one and obviously does not belong exclusively to the Cistercian aesthetic, nor is it limited to Christian thinking.

Cistercian concern for order is distinguished by its clarity and transparency. The unadorned structures emphatically display the principles of balance, rhythm, repetition, and the proportionality of related shapes and spaces. Like the simple shapes, the principle of order has symbolic power as well as functional effectiveness. Whereas in some religious buildings the figural ornamentation veils, even obscures, architectural composition, Cistercian buildings radiate the beauty of measure and celebrate the relationship of parts to whole. This exaltation of order is witnessed both by the architecture and by their life and discipline.

---

[35] Peter Berger, *A Rumor of Angels* (Garden City, NY: Doubleday, 1970), p. 53.

Art historians have tended to relate the writings of Pseudo-Dionysius to the aesthetic espoused by the Abbot of St. Denis. Yet the same theologian can help us appreciate the aniconic aesthetic exemplified by Cistercian architecture. In *The Divine Names* Dionysius, writing of "appropriate symbols for things divine," selected light as his principal example:

> And what shall I say concerning the sun's rays considered in themselves? From the Good comes the light which is an image of goodness; wherefore the Good is described by the name of "Light," being the archetype thereof which is revealed in that image.[36]

Light, as a mystical symbol of the divine, transcendent God, illumines all being. It bestows meaning upon the highest, most perfect forms to the lowest; still, it is beyond them all. Superior to them, at the same time it keeps all in its embrace, creating, vitalizing, and retaining all being. Dionysius also suggests other symbols which can lend themselves equally well to abstract aesthetic forms such as measure, numerical principle, order, and simplicity.[37]

While light is a symbol common to both the iconic and the aniconic aesthetic, so also are order and unity in complexity. Architectural elements, however, devoid of images, can express these abstract symbols in a powerful way. Moreover, an austere clarity and simplification were at times requisites for mystical contemplation, as Dionysius pointed out:

> Now when the mind, through the things of sense, feels an eager stirring to mount toward spiritual con-

---

[36] Dionysius the Areopagite, *The Divine Names and The Mystical Theology*, trans. C. E. Rolt (London: S.P.C.K., 1972), p. 91.

[37] *Ibid.*, pp. 91ff.

Visible Image and Invisible Faith

> templations, it values most of all those aids from its perceptions which have the plainest form, the clearest words, the things most distinctly seen, because, when the objects of sense are in confusion, the senses themselves cannot present their message truly to the mind.[38]

This passage is especially instructive, suggesting that unadorned, distinct forms have particular value for contemplation.

A deeper dimension of the visual language of the imageless aesthetic is suggested when, in *The Mystical Theology*, we read of the renunciation of the self and of all things so that in purity the self is led upwards to the "ray of that divine Darkness which exceedeth all existence." Through stripping away, through the purification of the tangible, one ascends to unity with God. Emptiness, silence, even bewilderment—in Dionysius' words, the "darkness of unknowing"—characterize the journey by which the medieval mystic was united with the One who is wholly unknowable. In their passion for simplicity the Cistercian builders developed an architectural expression of the awesome beauty and emptiness of the *via negativa*. The stark forms are a fitting context for the "true initiate into the darkness of unknowing" who, renouncing understanding, "is enwrapped with that which is wholly intangible and invisible...beyond all things."[39]

While Pseudo-Dionysius may be called upon to help us reflect upon Cistercian architecture, we should remember that builders—mastermasons and architects—create these monuments and that symbolic associations are frequently subjective.

---

[38] *Ibid.*, p. 103.

[39] *Ibid.*, p. 194.

More important, the Cistercian transformations of twelfth-century architecture and their development of an aniconic aesthetic are fundamentally rooted in the commitment of Bernard and his followers to utter simplicity and to poverty.[40]

It is important also to remember that the spare, mathematical beauty of these Cistercian churches was enlivened by liturgy and humanized by the literary forms. A rich verbal symbolism—stories, allegories, sermons, the reading and interpretation of Scripture—replaced the visual narratives of Vézelay. In his study of monastic culture, *The Love of Learning and the Desire for God*, Jean Leclercq comments on the relationship between literary pursuits and the monks' mystical life. He cites Bernard as the supreme example of the way in which "under the action of God, literature and the mystical life become one, to the point of being inseparable." Neither the Cistercian literary nor architectural styles, however, could be considered "art for art's sake." Instead, their art emerged from their spiritual life—their vows of poverty, their zeal for simplicity, and their commitment to God.[41]

Although their attitudes toward images indicate different assumptions and interests, the aims of Suger and Bernard were similar. In neither of these medieval thinkers was there any sign of a gnostic tendency to locate evil in material substance. Each in his own way transformed cultural forms to express and shape religious communication. Since their aesthetic gifts, sensibilities and communities differed, they chose contrasting media to witness to and awaken the life of the spirit. As we have seen, Suger selected the most precious objects and images to enhance the li-

---

[40] Peter Fergusson, *Architecture of Solitude: Cistercian Abbeys in Twelfth-Century England* (Princeton: Princeton University Press, 1984), p. 101.

[41] Jean Leclercq, O.S.B., *The Love of Learning and the Desire for God*, trans. Catherine Misrahi (New York: Fordham University Press, 1961), p. 317.

Visible Image and Invisible Faith

turgical setting. Committed to poverty and simplicity, Bernard and his followers ruled out such adornment. Still, both twelfth-century men were leaders for whom Christ became a transformer of culture. The ascetic Bernard has indeed been described as "a poet, a creator." To put the artist Bernard in perspective, Leclercq has written that the "extreme frontiers of literature...open into the whole realm of the ineffable." But even for Bernard the word of God yielded to the inexpressible. Leclercq quotes Bernard as saying, "What takes place between God and me, I can feel, but not express. When with you, on the contrary, I try to speak in a way that you will understand." Yet in the same passage Bernard cautions, " Prepare not your ear but your soul; for it is grace that teaches it and not language."[42] Suger's concerns may be understood in similar ways. The visual arts are used as a means to communicate on a human plane, to lead persons toward the vision of God, but they are not the vision itself. The bond between Suger and Bernard was their common concern for liturgy. While differing in their attitudes toward particular arts, they were equally passionate in appropriating cultural forms for use in public prayer and worship. Suger's ultimate defense of the arts was that they serve the mystery of the eucharist. Bernard's monks, in their worship, contributed poems, hymns, reflections, and sermons. It was indeed through liturgy, Leclercq notes, that all human resources attained their final potential and were offered to God in homage and in recognition of the source. "In the liturgy," he writes, "love of learning and the desire of God find perfect reconciliation."[43]

---

[42] *Ibid.*, pp. 328-329.

[43] *Ibid.*, p. 308.

Triumph of the Image

In the Middle Ages the use of images became widespread throughout Christendom. While Cistercian functional forms contributed to the development of Gothic architecture, Bernard's strictures ultimately had little impact outside the order. Even there, the design of later churches was less severe and in time the Cistercians became almost indistinguishable from other monastic groups in the church. By the thirteenth century the iconic aesthetic reigned supreme. Gothic churches, especially in northern Europe, achieved unprecedented visual splendor. Stained glass, ornament, and statuary within the sanctuary and architectural sculpture on the exterior mirrored Suger's confidence in the ability of images and objects to inspire devotion and nurture the faith of the laity.

In their theological statements medieval churchmen reinforced and extended earlier positions which justified the use of images for particular purposes. Their arguments generally followed the line of reasoning established by Gregory the Great: images provided a narrative of biblical history and religious instruction for the unlearned, just as reading the Old and New Testaments enabled the educated to learn about their faith from the Scriptures. In addition, these images were considered a tangible, visible aid to devotion and contemplation. In this connection Thomas Aquinas spoke of the "double character" of the movement of the soul toward the image. The soul, he said, moves toward the image insofar as it is an inanimate carved or painted object. At the same time, the soul is attracted to the image because it represents a reality other than itself. But, like Pope Gregory, Aquinas emphasized that *no veneration at all* is offered to the image itself—the carving or painted surface. Through the image or object the devout person may express devotion, not to the object, but to that to which the symbol refers. When the representation points beyond itself to Christ, it

Visible Image and Invisible Faith

is Christ who is venerated.[44] As aids to instruction and devotion, visual symbols became an integral part of medieval culture.

While many examples of medieval religious statuary, paintings and representational ornament can be seen today in museums all over the world, in their day they were not "art" as we now think of it. As Johann Huizinga observed in *The Waning of the Middle Ages*, the objects were not regarded simply for their beauty:

> Art in those times was still wrapped up in life....Life was encompassed and measured by the rich efflorescence of the liturgy: the sacraments, the canonical hours of the day and the festivals of the ecclesiastical year....The task of art was to adorn all these concepts with charm and colour; it is not desired for its own sake, but to decorate life with the splendour which it could bestow.[45]

Perhaps no monument in western architecture and art expresses this richness as powerfully as the French cathedral at Chartres. The modern photographer Charles Scheeler noted in his journal that this cathedral so overwhelmed and awed him that it was several days before he could summon courage to try to photograph it. The south portal, for example, when viewed from a distance, shimmers in architectural majesty with rich textural surfaces. But, as one moves closer and closer to the facade, it becomes clear that this eloquent unity is actually composed of innumerable parts. A composite of individuality in detail and wholeness in design, it suggests the theological mys-

---

[44] Bevan, *Holy Images*, p. 150-151.

[45] Johann Huizinga, *The Waning of the Middle Ages* (Garden City, NY: Doubleday, 1956), p. 244.

tery of the One and the many. The architectural forms and representational images in glass and stone at Chartres characterize what the late Sir Kenneth Clark referred to as the sacramental function of the arts: the capacity of material elements to render visible the immaterial and invisible ideals and beliefs of a people.[46] In our secular and technological society, such images should be understood not as art, but as sacramental objects.

In developing arguments for the use of images Paulinus of Nola, Gregory the Great, Thomas Aquinas, and others were recognizing the persistent human need for aids in approaching and symbolizing transcendent reality. While their historical perspectives differed, all were attempting to clarify the role of visible and concrete symbols in Christian pedagogy and devotion and to make important distinctions between the material representation and the divine reality it symbolized. Yet such distinctions often became blurred, particularly in the popular piety of the uneducated and unsophisticated. Thus to some religious leaders the proliferation of objects amidst splendid liturgical spaces was excessive, an undue accommodation of the human inclination to seek the sacred through the concrete.

The Protestant Challenge

The extravagance of medieval Catholic culture became a common concern of sixteenth-century reformers. Their reforms were more radical and pervasive than those of Bernard and the Cistercians, whose objections to images had long been overshadowed by the grandeur of late Gothic art and architecture. The Protestant Reformation came with such force that the iconic aesthetic itself was shattered along with cathedral images.

---

[46] Kenneth Clark, "Art and Society," in *The Nature of Art*, John Gassner and Sidney Thomas, eds. (New York: Crown, 1964), pp. 60, 64.

Visible Image and Invisible Faith

For Martin Luther the arts were important for instruction and
as aids to devotion, and in this respect he stood apart from other
reformers. The disagreements can be seen clearly in the conflict
with his colleague Andreas Carlstadt, who rejected both church
music and religious images as distractions, and, most important
of all, interpreted the sacraments of the eucharist as purely spiritual. The key issue in this dispute, underscored by historian Roland Bainton, was Carlstadt's disparagement of all material objects as aids to devotion. Bainton singles out the essential clue
to Luther's attitude toward the arts; for Luther, the spirit and
flesh were never disjoined. In his devotions, he was "aided by
the sight of the crucifix, the sound of the anthems, and the par-
taking of the body of Christ upon the altar."[47] Thus Luther
maintained a sacramental view of the unity of flesh and spirit,
acknowledging the mystery of the relationship between the visible and the invisible. And as Luther's reformation proceeded in
Germany, his followers did not deface or destroy the art and architecture they took over. Moreover, for Luther the liturgy
offered new dimensions in musical expression.

The most far-reaching aesthetic transformations arose through
the influence of John Calvin and Ulrich Zwingli, whose reforms
went beyond Luther's. Calvin rejected all images as aids to
devotion—even the crucifix—and permitted only a simple
cross. Although he allowed the congregation to sing psalms,
Scripture was the primary guide and aid to devotion. Zwingli,
for his part, rejected both music and images. Although he himself was a talented musician, who from an early age had shown
great interest in music, he ultimately eliminated it from liturgy.

Zwingli formulated his most complete arguments against images late in 1524 or early in 1525 in a document entitled, "An

---

[47] Roland H. Bainton, *Christendom: A Short History of Christianity and Its Impact on
Western Civilization* (New York: Harper & Row, 1966), 2:25.

Answer to Valentine Compar." He builds his case against his critic Compar on the distinction he makes between true and false Christian belief. The true believer, said Zwingli, is one who trusts God alone as an absolute and unconditional good. since the true believer knows that help, protection, grace, death and life rest solely in God's hands, there is no need to erect another "father, helper, solacer, or protector." Anything or any person placed between God and self encourages idolatry. Zwingli consistently used the term "strange god" in describing the psychic process that occurs in one's interior life when something or someone displaces God at the center of existence.[48]

Such "strange gods" included not only images but also wealth, power, prestige, possessions—anything that directs one away from God. Those familiar with H. Richard Niebuhr's *Radical Monotheism and Western Culture* will recognize in Zwingli's position one expression of a strident monotheism centered in God alone. All idolatry originates in the human tendency to place ultimate confidence and loyalty in material objects or some cause other than God. An important additional factor, however, is Zwingli's sympathy toward a kind of Platonic dualism which tended to devalue the material world. Thus, unlike Luther, he rejected the cultural homage that medievalists brought to the eucharistic mystery and so desacralized all material elements as aids to devotion.[49] Zurich's churches became highly rationalized, functional spaces in which liturgy consisted

---

[48] Charles Garside, Jr., *Zwingli and the Arts* (New Haven: Yale University Press, 1966), pp. 163-166.

[49] In this respect historians have emphasized the profound effects of Erasmus' thought on Zwingli's views. Although he never broke with the Catholic church, Erasmus had a tendency to dematerialize and rationalize worship; in Zwingli's thought, a similar pattern developed.

Visible Image and Invisible Faith

essentially of the preaching and hearing of the word of God. "Faith," writes Zwingli, "is from the invisible God, and is something completely apart from all that is sensible. Anything that is body, anything that is of the sense cannot be an object of faith." After all the images were removed and the churches whitewashed, he found them to be positively luminous: "the walls are beautifully white."[50] Thus all of the arts that had for centuries witnessed to Christian faith were unequivocally rejected.

Although the Cistercian aesthetic arose from an interest in simplification, it was not a denial of form and materiality. As we have seen, its concrete elements—light, pure geometric shapes, and the composition of those forms—were a material expression of their monastic commitments. Cistercian architectural style contrasted sharply with the imagistic Romanesque and Gothic churches; nevertheless, both the iconic and aniconic aesthetics of Catholic Christianity emphasized the centrality of the eucharist. Each was dependent upon the concrete engagement of worshipers with material elements; both confirmed mysterious connections in the sacraments between the finite and the infinite. The radical reshaping of liturgy by Zwingli, however, denied any such sacramental relationship; materiality and faith were separated. The believer was oriented to God solely by faith and Scripture. Christian worship centered not on the eucharist but on the reading, hearing, and interpretation of the Bible. Emptied of visual images, liturgical space became a place in which preaching and the reading of Scripture were paramount.

In his efforts to root out what he considered idolatry, Zwingli developed an anti-sacramental theology which demystified the unity of flesh and spirit. The separation of the expression of

---

[50] Garside, p. 160.

faith from material substance was complete, and even the starting point of the *via negativa* was lost. Moreover, this severely rational, imageless liturgy was imposed on the whole community of believers, lay and ordained. Eventually, music was reintroduced into Zurich's churches, but the theology and liturgy of the Swiss reformer dramatically changed the relationship between Protestant artists and religious institutions.

This tradition had important repercussions for the visual arts and their role in society. In predominantly Protestant countries that adhered closely to the theology of Calvin and Zwingli, there was little or no liturgical work for artists in the centuries that followed. The seventeenth-century Dutch painter, Rembrandt, for example, frequently used religious subjects in his paintings and etchings, but there was no place for them in the churches of seventeenth-century Holland. His Flemish contemporary Peter Paul Rubens, on the other hand, moved in royal circles and was sought out for his elaborate decoration of Baroque churches in Roman Catholic countries throughout Europe. In the absence of any such demand for church art in Holland, there grew up instead an unprecedented and rich tradition of genre, landscape, still-life, and portraiture—types of painting which depended almost exclusively upon patronage outside the church.

Thus far we have briefly traced the functions of the visual arts as purveyors of religious meaning as Christian culture assimilated two contradictory aesthetics: the aniconic tradition of Judaism and the iconic conventions of the classical world. Over time the figural, visual language observed on ancient monuments—friezes and statuary, for example—was continually transformed by Christian artisans and served a number of functions. Like ancient visual narratives, the carved images at Vézelay and Chartres helped to define the status quo and to legitimate the prevailing social order, reminding believers of what values they should emulate. In the Middle Ages visual im-

Visible Image and Invisible Faith

ages instructed the unlettered in both Scripture and doctrine; in the liturgy they served as aids to devotion and the nurture of faith.

The asceticism of the radical reformers had a marked influence on the role of the visual arts in church and culture, and this influence extended to the New World, particularly in New England, where Protestant settlers laid a foundation for a new relationship between invisible faith and visible forms. In the next chapter we will examine how the arts flourished—or floundered—as individual artists sought to use their work as a vehicle of religious communication in nineteenth-century America. In the absence of a public function, the visual arts assumed, especially in the later twentieth-century, a formidable role in the shaping of private meanings.

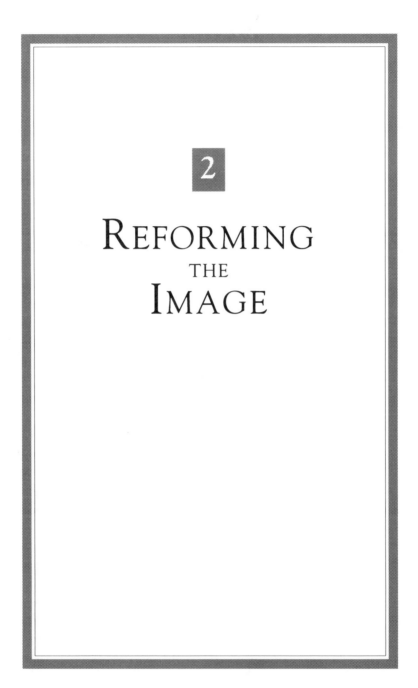

2

REFORMING
THE
IMAGE

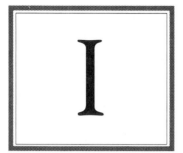magine Zwingli and Calvin in a seventeenth-century New England meeting house. These formidable clergymen are probably pleased with what they see. They approve the interior space, oriented to a pulpit which is centered and elevated above the pews in order to dramatize the ascendancy of the word of God. In Europe, before their reforms revolutionized worship and the design of churches, the altar dominated the space while the long nave stretching toward it enhanced its importance. By contrast, the New England meeting house is generally wider than it is long. Some are square, and often galleries are added for larger congregations. The construction is simple, with no attempt at elaboration or decoration, while the walls, plain and unadorned, are patterned by a flood of bright light coming through a spacious array of windows of clear glass. As in their own reformed churches, the two visitors observe neither painting nor sculpture in the liturgical space. It strikes them that these American worshipers share with them and with St. Paul the conviction that the only icon of the invisible God is Jesus Christ. And they understand, too, that God is revealed primarily through the enlivening word of the Scriptures.

In the time of the reformers, churches in Geneva and Zurich had to be whitewashed and images removed, but in New England there was no legacy of medieval art and architecture to reform. Puritan settlers could start afresh to build with principles similar to those established by the earlier reformers. In their British homeland, terrible conflicts arose when they attempted to modify the older Anglican church buildings. When they arrived in the New World, the immigrants rejoiced that they could build worship spaces in the woodlands and make a new society without being encumbered by the artistic traditions of

Reforming the Image

the established church or royalty. They could develop a society that conformed to their religious principles. The absence of a lavish material culture in America was for them a positive gain.

Nevertheless, the New England Puritans lacked neither aesthetic imagination nor appreciation of the material world. In this they resembled those earlier reformers, the Cistercians. For both, the beauty of simple interiors was enhanced by light, geometric elements, and elegant proportions. Denied visual representations as aids to worship, these New Englanders found ways, as one historian has put it, "to satisfy the universal craving for well-wrought mimesis. Having outlawed the satisfactions of high-church ritual (a form of dance and drama) and fearful of the magnetic attractions of icons and idolatry, they turned to literature."[1] Spiritual autobiography, sermons, and essays blossomed with figurative imagery, demonstrating a rich symbolism and emotional energy that was rooted in the Puritans' religious experience and regard for this new land.

Neither Zwingli nor Calvin, however, would have objected to painting and sculpture outside the worship space. Calvin, for example, thought the visual arts might be useful in narrating important human events. Their rejection of art was aimed essentially at its use as aids for devotion and the enhancement of churches. New England churches, empty of painting and sculpture, had adopted the principles of Calvin and Zwingli. When, later on, the simple, straightforward plan of the meeting house was replaced by more sophisticated designs and styles, the aniconic tradition remained firmly entrenched in most Protestant denominations. Although art was viewed positively, it was generally considered unsuitable for liturgical space.

---

[1] Norman S. Grabo, "The Veiled Vision: The Role of Aesthetics in Early American Intellectual History," in Sacvan Bercovitch, ed., *The American Puritan Imagination* (London: Cambridge University Press, 1974), p. 24.

In the early years of American culture it was difficult for artists to find work. Outside of portraiture and the decorative and serviceable arts, they found few demands for their profession in predominantly Protestant sections of the country. In the early nineteenth century, however, several American artists sought a vital place for the visual arts appropriate for this nation's religious and democratic principles. During this century there also began to emerge changing conceptions of the nature and function of religious art and symbolism.

In this chapter I want to trace the outlines of a reformulation of religious art in American society. The contours of this change may be detected in the work and thought of several nineteenth and twentieth century painters. By highlighting their concerns we can see how the artist became increasingly responsible for the content as well as for the form of religious symbolism. Ancient and medieval painters and sculptors, by contrast, were not expected to create the myths to which they gave visible expression. Following the Reformation, however, artists with religious interests began to assume the burden of myth-making as well as image-making.[2] This evolution is particularly apparent in the ethos of a nineteenth-century Protestant piety. Here I have chosen only those artists who left written records—journals, articles, letters—reflecting their specific religious interests. As statements by twentieth-century artists are more enigmatic and cryptic, I have concentrated on those whose work has been assigned religious import by critics.

Some nineteenth-century artists—Washington Allston and Thomas Cole, for example—wished to paint stories from the

---

[2] See Robert Rosenblum, *Modern Painting and the Northern Romantic Tradition: Friedrich to Rothko* (New York: Harper & Row, 1975). Rosenblum has charted a fundamental, persistent search of northern Romantic painters for non-traditional symbols to express religious experience.

Reforming the Image

Bible or mythology, but most people had little interest in explicit religious themes. The public was more fascinated with subject matter drawn from the ordinary world and from nature. At the same time, however, these artists had a religious view of nature that contributed significantly to their vision of art and to the communication of spiritual knowledge. In their paintings and writings we are able to trace a gradual liberation from traditional concepts of religious art. By the end of the nineteenth century religious symbolism was no longer confined to conventional sacred stories but was found by some artists in landscape and nature images. Later, during the twentieth century, a number of artists and theorists believed religious meaning could best be expressed in abstract forms. Along with this freedom of interpretation, however, there was a consequent shift in the burden of meaning from the icon itself to the private religious imagination of the artist or viewer. By the last decade of the century, the practice of art represented for some a spiritual odyssey and personal search for meaning; for pious viewers the works of such artists became objects of contemplation.

Nature: A Source of Religious Revelation

Over the centuries nature has evoked religious wonder and served as inspiration for artists. By the nineteenth century, nature assumed special importance in America as a source of religious revelation, as God's "other book." Seen as disclosing essential truths, it became, like the Bible, a reservoir of iconography.[3] Williams examines views of nature that have appeared throughout Christian culture, including nature as a source of religious revelation. For the Puritans, the Bible was still the major source of revelation and typology. A hermeneutical device, ty-

---

[3] See George H. Williams, "Christian Attitudes Toward Nature," *Christian Scholar's Review* 2:1:3-35; 2:2:112-126.

pology was one way that theologians of the early church related the Old and New Testaments, whereby historical events and spiritual heroes of the Hebrew Scriptures were seen to prefigure the events of the New Testament and the saving work of Christ. Similarly, early American settlers saw themselves as a new chosen people and interpreted the wilderness as a New Eden.

Just when nature emerged as a source of revelation and typology in American religion is less clear. Scholars have found in the writings of Samuel Mather only hints of nature's revelatory power, and for Jonathan Edwards, although types existed in nature, the basic patterns of interpretation were scriptural. Nevertheless, it has been observed that Edwards was extraordinarily sensitive to nature, more so than others of his time. The description of Edwards' conversion in his *Personal Narrative* offers a remarkable verbal picture of nature seen through the eyes of one transformed. He recalled his first delight in God upon reading 1 Timothy 1:17, "Now unto the King Eternal, immortal, invisible, the only wise God, be honor and glory forever and ever, Amen." Following this experience the young Edwards walked alone in his father's pasture in contemplation:

> And as I was walking there, and looking upon the sky and clouds, there came unto my mind so sweet a sense of the glorious *majesty* and *grace* of God, as I know not how to express....The appearance of every thing was altered; there seemed to be, as it were, a calm, sweet cast or appearance of divine glory, in almost everything. God's excellency, his wisdom, his purity, and love, seemed to appear in every thing; in the sun, moon, and stars; in the clouds and blue sky; in the grass, flowers, trees; in the water and all nature.[4]

---

4 *The Works of Jonathan Edwards*, 2 vols. (Edinburgh: The Banner of Truth Trust, 1979), 1:1:xiii

Reforming the Image

Revelation through Nature did not assume a prominent place in American theology until the nineteenth century. It was Ralph Waldo Emerson who formulated for his contemporaries an appropriate theology. Nature's serene order, he said, is "the present expositor of the divine mind" and cannot be violated by human hands. We are strangers in nature and, in fact, know very little about its creatures and innermost workings. "We do not understand the notes of birds....We do not know the uses of more than a few plants." Occasionally our contemplation of nature is disturbed by people; if laborers, he explains, are digging in a nearby field, we cannot freely admire the noble land.[5]

When we try to describe God, Emerson went on to say, language and thought fail us because spiritual essence resists words and propositions. Nature, however, may stand as the "apparition" of God. It is the great "organ through which the universal spirit speaks to the individual, and strives to lead back the individual to it." In a chapter entitled "Spirit," from his book *Nature*, Emerson posed a question: "Is not the landscape, every glimpse of which had a grandeur, a face of Him?" Emerson was, of course, referring to one's physical presence in nature—standing in solitude beside a lake, alone in the woodlands, observing the clarity of the stars on a winter's night. It is easy to see, however, that for an artist interested in religious symbols another question might arise: If nature reveals religious truth, could not the *image* of such grandeur also awaken a consciousness of Spirit? Could it become a religious icon? It would seem that the glory of God, which to Edwards "seemed to appear in every thing," could be visualized in the brilliant colors and forms of a landscape painting.

---

[5] Ralph Waldo Emerson, *Nature* (San Francisco: Chandler, 1968), p. 81.

When Emerson's essay was published in 1836, landscape painting had already become very popular. Yet two American painters who were seriously concerned with religious art, Thomas Cole and Washington Allston, were still pursuing religious themes based on biblical or allegorical narrative. It was not until twenty years later that Cole's friend Asher B. Durand, identified landscape painting with a theology of nature. Nevertheless, these three painters contributed, each in a different way, to a reformulation of religious art in a Protestant ethos and to the creation of a public role for the visual image. They each found a formal language for fulfilling about the sacramental function of art, its capacity for making visible human beliefs and values.

Thomas Cole, widely acclaimed as a landscapist, was also a poet and essayist who kept a detailed journal. His writings, together with his paintings, show the hopes, expectations and frustrations of a painter who wanted to produce art that was religious. Cole was a traditionalist who believed that art fulfilled an important function in churches. Even though people no longer had to depend upon pictures for learning Christian doctrines, he was convinced that painting and sculpture could perform a teaching role. Recalling the place of images in early Christianity, he suggested that nineteenth-century Protestants visit the catacombs to learn about the early consecration of art. Principles that guided Christian art and architecture through the centuries could still meet current needs, Cole argued, and he sharply criticized the church for rejecting painting and sculpture. If American artists were not at work for the church, it was not, he said, that they lacked the capacity for important religious art, only that they lacked opportunity.

Reforming the Image

On the other hand, Cole was pessimistic about church or government patronage. Many Americans, he said, think of the arts merely as "pleasurable toys."[6] Though most people can easily understand the need for government assistance for the useful arts, they tend to think of the fine arts as simply amusing, even corrupting. Both church and government, he concluded, can be served by the visual arts, especially by their power to inspire and instruct. Serviceable arts and utilitarian forms contribute to the well-being of a society, but they do not meet its spiritual needs. That was, in Cole's view, the responsibility of the fine arts.

Cole did not, however, find institutional support for his work. His earliest successes were paintings of the countryside. Even then he wrote of his aspirations for a "higher type of landscape"[7] that would narrate a moral or religious truth. Along with his views, Cole exhibited landscapes based on traditional biblical themes, such as *The Garden of Eden* and *Expulsion from the Garden of Eden*.

In the *Expulsion from the Garden of Eden* (1827-28), the story is told almost entirely through the elements of landscape. When viewed from a distance, the painting appears to be a dramatic composition of light and dark. Rays of light break through an opening in the center of the composition to illuminate the garden, a light area isolated by a rocky chasm of great depth. Animals and birds inhabit the garden, where luxuriant vegetation and graceful trees confirm the peace, plenty, and innocence of Eden. Dividing the composition is the gate through which Adam and Eve have been driven after eating from the tree of

---

[6] Thomas Cole, Unpublished notes. "Lecture" (on the "Arts of Design"), Cole Papers, New York State Library, Albany, NY, p. 13.

[7] Louis Legrand Noble, *The Life and Works of Thomas Cole* (Cambridge, MA: Harvard University Press, 1964), pp. 64, 203.

knowledge. The only light that leaves Eden comes from the flaming sword that guards the gate to the garden. Crossing over into the world of toil and death, Adam and Eve confront dark forms whose rugged, torn contours are illuminated only by the light from the portal. Instead of the magnificence of Eden, they walk into a grotesque landscape in which all the elements attack each other. Trees are ravished and uprooted by storms. Stags that leapt playfully in Eden are now being devoured by a beast, while a vulture awaits the remains. The cactus has replaced the lotus, the light is generated only by nature's disturbances—a volcano and a lightning bolt in the far distance. Although the human plight is central to the biblical myth, here Adam and Eve are very small figures. Natural forms have assumed the principal role in this visual narration.

In a letter to one of his supporters, Cole described what he wanted to accomplish in his more serious landscapes and explained that he had priced them higher because of the great labor and study which went into them. Several elaborate allegorical landscapes were commissioned. For example, *The Course of Empire* (1836), a series of five large paintings, depicts the rise and fall of civilization—from its primitive state through its development, consummation, and ultimate destruction. It illustrated, for Cole, the transience of civilization. The artist's literary friends—James Fenimore Cooper was one—especially appreciated his symbolic landscapes. Cooper referred to this series as "one of the noblest works of art that has ever been wrought."[8]

In 1839 Cole received a commission to begin work on another visual allegory which he hoped would make a strong

---

8 *Ibid.*, p. 167.

Reforming the Image

"moral and religious impression."[9] Based on a long poem which he himself had composed, this series was entitled *The Voyage of Life*. The poem and paintings depict the spiritual pilgrimage of life in four stages: *Childhood*, *Youth*, *Manhood*, and *Old Age*. Again Cole uses the elements of landscape to portray the human condition. Mountainous recesses in the first painting, *Childhood*, signify the mysterious boundaries of life. From a deep cavern flows the stream of life on which glides a boat with an angel at the helm. The boat, filled with flowers, carries an infant. Only one bank of the stream is visible, indicating the limited horizon of childhood. Brilliant light illuminates a plain which extends from the base of the mountains. On it are small trees and blossoming foliage; the tree of life is just beginning to grow.

The next three paintings in this series trace the voyage through youth, manhood, and old age. Each landscape expresses changing human experiences. In *Youth* the stream of life has widened and the tree has matured. The larger horizon of experience is represented by both banks of the stream; the future is suggested by the distant background, revealing hopes and dreams. As the angel watches from the shore, the young man has taken over the helm of the boat. The mood is one of anticipation and exuberance. In the third painting, *Manhood*, it has changed to trepidation. The stream of life that once spread before the young man is now behind him. Cole's stormy skies, treacherous rocks, and contorted trees recall the world into which Adam and Eve were driven from paradise. The helm of the boat has been destroyed; the voyager faces swifter rapids and more dangerous shoals ahead. In the last painting, *Old Age*, the boat, without prow or helm, drifts away from the last barren

---

9   *Ibid.*, p. 203.

rocks of the shore. Landscape, the chronicler of mortality, has receded into the past. The stream of life which originated in the recesses of the dark cavern has flowed into the ocean of infinitude. Above, the guardian angel reappears and directs the voyager toward immortal life.

Like *The Course of Empire*, this series was admired by Cole's literary friends. William Cullen Bryant praised its imaginative qualities. Simpler and less elaborate in design than the earlier series, it was, he said, a perfect poem. Meanwhile, Cole continued to produce the landscapes for which he is best remembered. He referred to these more popular and marketable landscapes as his "views"; they were his chief means of support.

Cole wrote somewhat despairingly in his journal about undertaking a large landscape that would sell better than his "fancy pictures."[10] Yet this painting, The *Oxbow* (1836), is rich in symbolic overtones and, in its own way, reveals Cole's deep feelings for nature. The dominant spatial division of the painting is diagonal, running from the top left part of the painting to the lower right corner, dividing the landscape into two different types of terrain. On the left is the wild, untamed earth cherished by the painter. On the right, one can see the land cleared, cultivated, and domesticated. Cole was meticulous in detailing both sections. Farmland and pastures depicted on the right are carefully patterned by hedgerows, reflecting the geometry of agrarian and pastoral stewardship. Cole paints small groups of animals grazing and punctuates the valleys with dwellings which exude tiny trails of smoke from the chimneys; cleared fields extend into the distant horizon. On the left, freely growing natural forms are thick and luxuriant, governed only by the forces of nature itself—by storms and the winnowing of the seasons.

---

10 *Ibid.*, p. 159.

Reforming the Image

In this painting Cole has identified with nature by painting himself at work, nestled within its wilder part. Some of his equipment remains on the ledge overlooking the valley, and the painter seems to have moved deep into the wilderness. Above are the whirling, threatening clouds of a storm, but the real threat to Cole's beloved untrampled terrain is to be seen in the lower right hand corner of the painting. Although this detail is quite small, Cole has carefully depicted a flat boat setting out from the riverbank of the cultivated land. Aboard is a homesteading family, with its livestock and possessions, headed for the wilder area. Juxtaposed are the painter—conservator of the wilderness—and those crossing the river to subdue and domesticate it.

While Cole referred to *The Oxbow* as a "view," one sees in it, as indeed in all of his landscapes, a profound understanding and appreciation of nature. The placement of a small self-portrait literally on the side of the wilderness underscores, as do his writings, his conserving, reverential attitude toward it. Even so, Cole did not wish to be considered a "mere leaf-painter," and he continually sought to develop a "higher conception" of landscape art.[11] This meant, as we have seen, a religious symbolism that included a narrative, story-telling component expressing some moral or religious theme. It might be taken from Scripture or myth, or from the poetic imagination of the artist.

We can better understand how Cole participated in the emerging reinterpretation of religious art by looking at his writings, which show unmistakably that his own experience in nature was a fundamental source of religious inspiration. In his "Essay on American Scenery," Cole wrote that in the presence

---

[11] *Ibid.*, p.195.

of nature the mind turns to God the creator. Amid grandeur and solitude it is cast into contemplation. As one gazes on the "pure creations of the Almighty," a religious calm moves through the spirit. He noted the special privilege of American artists surrounded by a pristine environment. "We are," he said, "still in Eden."[12]

It seems ironic to us that Cole, feeling as deeply as he did about nature, preferred his allegorical landscapes over his "views." Even though his deepest religious affections were evoked in the midst of nature, in his paintings a narrative theme seemed indispensable to his concept of religious art. Although he clearly underscored in his essays and journal the power of nature to evoke wonder and reverence, still he did not go so far as to say that his landscapes convey religious meanings. In a letter to an artist-critic Cole spoke only of landscape's "sentiment" as "tranquil" or "spirit-stirring," although he was continually striving in his major works to illustrate traditional religious themes. Just two years before he died, Cole noted in his journal that he longed to paint whatever his imagination dictated without worrying about financial losses. In this entry he also spoke enthusiastically of a series of five paintings he was just beginning. Its theme was "The Cross and the World." "I have no commission," he wrote, "...I will venture in faith and hope."[13]

Cole's synthesis of landscape painting and religious narrative suggests one way of interpreting religious art. His older contemporary, Washington Allston, who lacked Cole's direct engagement with nature, was more philosophical. Allston's essays

---

[12] Thomas Cole, "Essay on American Scenery," *The American Monthly Magazine* N.S. 1 (1836): 3, 12.

[13] Noble, *Thomas Cole*, p. 274.

Reforming the Image

about art and nature, which paralleled those of Emerson, came close to interpreting landscape as a religious symbol.

Like Cole, he was convinced that the visual arts were not a luxury but were necessary for religious revelation and the spiritual growth of the nation. He, too, preferred to paint subjects from the Bible and mythology. Widely regarded as one of America's most distinguished artists, Allston was offered a commission to do a painting for the rotunda of the Capitol at Washington, D.C. He turned down this opportunity when it became clear that he could not choose a biblical theme for that space.

If we read Allston's *Lectures on Art*, we find there a theology of nature that differs from Cole's. Allston presents the artist as a religious visionary, a seer—one "ordained for the evolution of the human spirit." He regarded profound soul-searching as indispensable to creative activity. Furthermore, he believed that the artist had a special responsibility to sound the depths of experience and, through this process, to discern the spirit in natural forms. After this metaphysical exploration the artist would be able to render visible the invisible essence of physical reality. The resulting works of art could draw viewers out of themselves and direct them to the mind's "true object," the infinite Creator.[14]

Allston's view on art and the artist were based largely on an idealized perception of nature. In his studies at the British Royal Academy, he was trained to think of nature as a generalization of individual forms. From observing many instances of, say, the branching of trees, the artist distills a representative or "ideal" image. The academician's approach contrasts with another that seeks to portray the particular—for example, a single cluster of branches with all its distinguishing, eccentric features. Until

---

[14] Washington Allston, *Lectures on Art and Poems*, ed. Richard H. Dana, Jr. (New York: Baker and Scribner, 1850), pp. 110, 74.

late in his career, when a more detailed treatment appears, the idealized view of nature dominates Allston's writings as well as his paintings.

At the same time his essays disclose a religious understanding of nature, one that harmonizes with Emersonian theology. When writing about the "idea" of nature, Allston is referring to a vital core in all living things. To him the universe was infused in all of its particular parts with a principle of infinite being. While for Cole nature inspired wonder and witnessed to God's handiwork, Allston went farther and found in nature rich opportunities to discern the divine essence present in all reality. Here, in some measure, is a return to the view of the medieval mystics that God is present in all aspects of the natural order. This idea also resonates with the romantic belief that nature is filled with the divine presence. Although Allston's speculations are Emersonian in tone, their source is not the famous Boston transcendentalist but another New England intellectual, James Marsh. An admirer of Samuel Taylor Coleridge, Marsh rekindled in Allston an earlier fascination with this philosopher-poet and also introduced the painter to German philosophers, among them F. H. Jacobi. In developing his own ideas and expressing them, Allston was heavily influenced by Marsh's terminology and theories.[15]

When it comes to relating Allston's theological idea of nature to his pictures, there are difficulties, for his writings came late in his career when his interest in painting was declining. Still, one characteristic of his work, a preoccupation with light, seems to link his practice with his theory. Among Allston's

---

[15] M. Gregor T. Goethals, "A Comparative Study of the Theory and Work of Washington Allston, Thomas Cole, and Horatio Greenough" (Ph.D. diss., Harvard University, 1966), pp. 48ff.

Reforming the Image

papers were found these sentences from German philosophy, painstakingly copied by the artist as follows:

> Only he who has contemplated the intelligible, spir-
> itual world, beyond and above the sphere of that
> which rises and sinks, comes into existence and then
> ceases to be. . . finds again the types and symbols of
> it in the world of sense. Only he knows that the uni-
> verse exists through the Good, which. . . has brought
> forth not only the knowledge of the truth, but the
> truth itself, like the sun, which not only gives light
> and visibility, but to the visible its life also; he only
> recognizes in this visible universe a creation, the
> work of a God.[16]

At the end of this transcription Allston added: "See Plato de Republica, end 6th book and beginning of the 7th." While he made no reference to this passage in his published essays, it shows the artist's interest in the Platonic use of light as a meta-phor for the source of both being and knowing, and it points the way toward interpreting light as a religious symbol.

Allston's paintings demonstrate a mixture of academic train-ing and romantic reverie. His landscapes, especially those in which light dominates, best express his affinity with the Pla-tonic metaphor. In *Moonlit Landscape* (1819), a luminous moon defines all the shapes in the painting. Mountains in the back-ground, seen against the brightness of the sky, separate earth and heaven. In the center of the composition, one mountain seems to direct us to the source of light, the moon; domes, whose shapes suggest an antique world, echo its contour. The semicircular structure of the bridge and reflections in the water bring light into the lower part of the painting, sharply silhouet-

---

[16] Washington Allston, Unpublished notes, "From Dr. Marsh's translation of Jacobi," Dana Collection, Allston Papers, Folder no. 17, Massachusetts Historical Society, Bos-ton, MA.

ting human figures. In the distance a lone figure and a small family group walk away from the shore, their backs to the light. Only a rider on horseback, facing the light, is in a position to contemplate the scene. Like the horseman, the observer views the patterns of reflected light and shadow. In this painting Allston has taken a classical scene he might have observed in seventeenth-century artists, such as Claude Lorraine or Nicholas Poussin, and reconstructed it through gradations of light which disclose and enliven the basic motifs of the painting.

Sixteen years later in *Landscape, Afternoon with Southwest Haze* (1835), natural forms are less generalized. Light now enables nature to be more transparent, revealing individual aspects of trees and foliage. Objects displaying their own special textures, shapes, and color suggest an animated nature. The passage of time is no longer symbolized through old-world architectural motifs. Instead we sense the transience of things through the particularity of light that records the time of day and the weathered tree that has withstood the passage of seasons. There is also in this painting a horseman; the rider no longer contemplates the scene but moves from a path into a stream that stretches across the entire painting. No space in the foreground allows the observer to view nature from a distance; instead, Allston has taken the viewer directly into nature.

The painter's written reflections on art suggest the possibility that landscape, or any subject, for that matter, might disclose a spiritual truth. Since all living things are animated by the divine "idea," an artist inspired by this insight may transform images of ordinary reality into icons. There is no evidence in his *Lectures on Art* that Allston ever realized the full implication of the philosophy of nature he had absorbed from Coleridge and Marsh; nevertheless, his paintings and writings point to important changes in the meaning of the term "religious artist." He was continually preoccupied with the creative process as an experience which led the artist, and ultimately the viewer, to a

Reforming the Image

greater awareness of spiritual truth. In his essays, and increasingly in his own paintings, he envisioned the artist as a solitary seeker of religious reality and considered that search to be a social responsibility. Yet with Allston we begin to see a shift in art from a corporate to a private religious function. Indeed, his solitary explorations, in a sense, prefigure those of his twentieth-century counterparts for whom art became a means of personal salvation.

Both Cole and Allston exemplify the disappointments and frustrations of early nineteenth-century American artists who wanted to create meaningful public symbols. In spite of their religious view of nature, neither fully understood that landscape painting itself might communicate religious meaning. The status of "religious painting" was first bestowed upon landscape by Cole's friend, Asher B. Durand. This idea he developed in a series of "Letters on Landscape Painting," which were printed in *The Crayon*, a leading art journal of his day. Durand enlarged the concept of religious symbols to include landscape painting, without, however, the philosophical language of Allston. Instead, Durand drew upon his own experiences as a painter and upon the religious attitudes toward nature that he shared with Cole. In his "Letters" the painter touched on many subjects, offering practical advice as well as religious interpretations of nature.

He urged artists interested in landscape to go to the "studio" of nature to learn its truthfulness and master the first principles of the true "religion of Art." Durand insisted that inexperienced painters observe closely its rich detail: the light that strikes the trunk of an oak; the color, texture, and lines of foliage; the gradations of light and dark that define space and volume. He advised them that only through careful study could they understand its "wondrous structure." Moreover, Nature is filled with "lessons of high and holy meaning, surpassed only by the light of Revelation."[17]

Seeing nature as a source of religious knowledge is not, of course, unique to Durand. We have seen that the attitude was shared by artists, New England transcendentalists, and others. Durand went further, however, in pointing out that landscape painting itself communicates religious insight. Landscape art, he says, is the "representation of the work of God in visible creation"—independent of human action.[18] While not systematically excluding them, he found human figures useful only if they harmonized with the religious sentiments evoked by inanimate nature. To him landscape painting was uniquely suited to draw attention to the awesome creative acts of God evident in the world of nature. In this respect it took its place alongside paintings that depict traditional biblical subjects. From Durand's perspective, Cole's "views" could be seen as religious symbols or icons.

Durand, in his later work, seemed to follow the precepts developed in the essays. In *Woodland Interior* (1855), painted the same year that his "Letters" were published, he concentrated on nature as it is, moving the observer deeply and directly into the source of revelation. Freed from literary schemes, the painter lavished his attention upon natural forms, using light in a way that suggests a mysterious spiritual illumination within. This painting is rich in textures—the moss over the rocks, the bed of the forest, detailed foliage. Such imaging of nature may, like nature itself, declare the glory of God.

At the time Durand's writings were published, a number of other painters were creating intimately detailed pictures of na-

---

17 Asher B. Durand, "Letters on Landscape Painting," *The Crayon* 1 (1855): 2, 34.

18 *Ibid.*, p. 354.

Reforming the Image

ture. Just how many shared his interpretation of landscape as re-ligious symbol is uncertain, but it is clear that Durand's reflec-tions freed the religious imagination from the confines of bibli-cal subject matter. His work and thought prepared the way for both artists and viewers to discover religious meaning in nature images.

Although landscape painting remained very popular in America throughout the nineteenth century, not many artists made explicit references to its religious significance. George Inness was one of the few, but his remarks are fragmentary. Like Allston, he was preoccupied with light as a metaphor for the spiritual essence of material being, but his inspiration was Swedenborg, for whom the light of the sun, a symbol of divine love, was the infinite source of all reason. For Inness, color, light, shadow, and space suggested "the invisible side of visible objects."[19] In his landscapes he worked with layers of colors whose interaction created evanescent, luminous effects. Details of the natural world—trees, fields, clouds—were veiled, and their simplified forms seemed to radiate a kind of inner light.

Aware of Inness's religious interests, viewers can easily as-sociate the luminosity in the paintings with his preoccupation with divine light. His rendering of forms suggests an animating spirit in all of the natural world. Although an admirer of both Cole and Durand, Inness had moved far away from Cole's con-cept of religious art. While all three artists were interested in re-ligious revelation through paintings, their approaches to re-ligious symbolism differed. Cole associated religious art with the explicit use of biblical references or traditional mythological themes. To be sure, he was inspired by nature and saw it as a unique witness to the creator God upon whom all being is de-

---

[19] Inness, George, Jr., *Life, Art, and Letters of George Inness* (New York: The Century Co., 1917), p. 169.

pendent. Yet, for Cole, views of nature were not in themselves sufficient to communicate religious meaning. His predilection for narrative scriptural sources and his orthodox piety did not permit him to accept landscape painting in itself as a religious icon. Inness was perhaps closer in his attitude to Durand who, as we have seen, thought that a landscape painting stripped of mythological and human references could still communicate a sense of religious wonder and awe and testify to the work of the Creator.

It is interesting to imagine these three artists standing before Inness's landscape painting, *Early Autumn*. Of the three, Cole would have the greatest trouble interpreting the pastoral landscape as a suitable expression of religious sentiment. The layers of paint which set all nature aglow would still require, from his perspective, a sacred story. However evanescent the forms, for Cole the pervasive light would not sufficiently define or explicate Christian beliefs. To Durand, on the other hand, the painting would express a religious response to the glory of creation. He might, however, question Inness's observation and rendering of natural elements, since in his "Letters" Durand had recommended that landscapists pay close attention to the details of nature. But to achieve the sense of an inner light that radiates from natural forms, Inness has concentrated instead on generalized shapes, allowing light and color to dominate. Transparent layers of oil glazes diffuse the particularities—precise leaf patterns, configurations of branches, eccentric contours of rocks—that make up the complex whole of nature.

This imaginary meeting illustrates some difficulties that might arise in interpreting landscape as a religious icon. Even painters with explicit spiritual concerns have differing views about form and content. Those without religious interests could ask still more questions. Is nature benign? Is the presence of God found in each and every aspect of the created world? Are there other kinds of divine action in the world? Is creation

Reforming the Image

judged? Redeemed? Even if we accept nature as a revelation of the divine, a theological understanding of creation and Creator is uncertain.

Clearly the burden of meaning is transferred from the icon to the viewer. As artists moved away from traditional or biblical iconography, viewers had to assume an increasing responsibility for the interpretation of symbols. It is true, of course, that subjective interpretations are inevitable and that we all see things differently, especially since non-discursive forms of communication do not lend themselves to unambiguous meanings. At the same time, however, traditionally established religious iconography sets certain broad parameters which direct and channel viewer's responses. In the religious atmosphere of nineteenth-century America, we might reasonably expect landscape painting to inspire pious sentiments in viewers. But, since most artists did not leave written evidence of their religious concerns, modern scholars can only speculate about the religious meanings landscape painting held for them.[20]

---

[20] Barbara Novak, *American Painting of the Nineteenth Century: Realism, Idealism, and the American Experience* (New York: Harper & Row, 1969), pp. 51, 97. Certain art historians have assigned religious symbolism to particular types of landscape art, even when the artists have not indicated specific religious interests. John I. H. Baur first called attention to a group of painters whose light-filled canvases were rich in detailed observations. He characterized the work of Fitz Hugh Lane and Martin Johnson Heade as "pantheistic realism," and coined the term "American Luminism" to describe painting in which nature was portrayed with exceptional intensity, sharpness, and luminosity. Heade's marsh scenes and haystacks, for example, exquisitely detail the passage of light at certain moments of time. His portrayal of light and disclosure of particular textures provide a new way of seeing the palpable world. Following Baur's clue and exploring the Luminists in great detail, Barbara Novak concludes that "American religion of the nineteenth century was found in the landscapes of the pantheist realists" (see p. 51).

Novak, in fact, extends the Luminist vision to include not only landscape but also genre, still life, and portraiture. For her, the religious attitude of these painters appears not only in their concern for light but also in careful attention to detail. These painters were extraordinarily meticulous in portraying the ordinary, bestowing upon them order and measure. The artist acts as a clarifying lens and allows the spectator "to confront the image more directly and immediately" (p. 97).

A Search for Essence

Efforts to assign religious significance to landscape painting become even more complex in twentieth-century America. In a secular, pluralistic environment, analogies between theologies and nature images are speculative. Even so, some critics have placed two twentieth-century painters of nature, Georgia O'Keeffe and Arthur G. Dove, in the tradition of artists in search of spiritual symbols. For this interpretation one has to move far beyond the concepts of religious symbolism first associated with American art. Thomas Cole, for example, would have to abandon his piety and concern for biblical narration to find a spiritual dimension in the barren bones and landscapes of O'Keeffe. He would have to expand his sense of the "religious" if he were to understand modern critics who discern in her work cosmological themes and a search for an essential principle of being.

In attributing religious symbolism to the works of O'Keeffe and Dove, critics have indeed found analogies for their works in the nature philosophy of both the nineteenth and twentieth centuries. Thus some critics, *not* the artists themselves, discern religious motifs in their works. While there are significant differences, the paintings of these two artists have been described as a search for the essential, an essence that is also an inner core of spirit. O'Keeffe's early experiments with pure line and color were followed by highly stylized cityscapes and flower

---

In developing her concept of the religious aspects of Luminist painting, Novak draws upon contemporary intellectual and religious traditions, particularly Emerson and the transcendentailists. Since these landscape painters left no documentary evidence to confirm their religious interests, Novak builds her interpretation upon correspondences, relating certain visual qualities in Luminist painting to Transcendentalist thought. She uses the language of Emerson to characterize the landscapes of Fitz Hugh Lane. For both the theologian and the painter "the universe becomes transparent, and the light of higher laws than its own shines through it" (see p. 122). Novak, aligning theology with painting styles and techniques, finds parallels that reinforce her hypothesis about the religious qualities of Luminism. By observing analogies between literary sources and art works, critics play a crucial role in assigning spiritual symbolism to ordinary subjects.

Reforming the Image

paintings. Later she turned to the barren, lean lines and colors of the desert, transforming and abstracting its elements into an intuitive, personal iconography. Some of these paintings appear almost entirely abstract, yet the metaphors of nature linger, manifested in the light, color and contours of her Taos sanctuary.

Similarly Dove's abstractions were distillations from nature—the rush of wind or the motion of water—sensations transposed into visual images. Like O'Keeffe, he experimented with abstraction, but seashore and storm, tilled field and orchard, sunrise and moonrise, however abstractly constructed, never disappear entirely from his paintings. His images hover in a delicate balance between the familiar natural world we perceive and the vital forms the artist discovers in them.

O'Keeffe and Dove both spoke of nature as a starting point in their search for the substance of natural forms. O'Keeffe commented: "From experience of one kind or another, shapes and colors come to me very clearly. Sometimes I start in a very realistic fashion and as I go on from one painting [to] another of the same thing, it becomes simplified till it can be nothing but abstract, but for me it is my reason for painting it, I suppose."[21] Dove's exploration of natural forms and search for their essence was a "delightful adventure." Farming and life on a houseboat brought a profound engagement with the forces of nature. In a letter to Stieglitz he wrote, "Have been trying to memorize this storm all day so that I can paint it. Storm green and storm grey. It's been too dark and nerve-straining to paint so did three il-

---

[21] John I. H. Baur, *Nature in Abstraction: The Relation of Abstract Painting and Sculpture to Nature in Twentieth-Century American Art* (Exhibition Catalogue published by the Whitney Museum of American Art, New York, 1958), p. 6.

lustrations this morning just to keep from cutting the rope through by thinking so hard about it." Sometimes his descriptions took on a mystical tone. He found a "condition of light" in all of nature—"flowers, people, apples, cows."[22] Dove's painting *Golden Storm* exemplifies his interest in sensation and its essential distillation. Through patterns of arcs he has transformed the eccentric, transitory experience of a storm into simplified shapes and colors. Yet these generalized, more universal visual elements can evoke in the mind's eye specific experiences. Abstracted shapes and colors combine to awaken recollections of swelling waves and the motion of blue-gray clouds, both tinged with the glow of light from a hidden sun.

Dove's interest in the elements of nature's processes have led some interpreters to look for religious or philosophical currents in his work. Art historian Barbara Haskell makes comparisons between Dove's image-making and the philosophy of Henri Bergson, whose ideas were circulated in Stieglitz's publication, *Camera Work*. For both the painter and the philosopher, she says, sympathetic response and intuitive engagement lead to the discovery of the unique and essential forms of life beyond the boundaries of the self.[23] Historian-critic Robert Rosenblum places both O'Keeffe and Dove in a long line of Romantic artists who sought to convey spiritual experience without using traditional religious subjects. In their transformation of natural phenomena O'Keeffe and Dove, he writes, have created "pic-

---

22 Frederick S. Wight, *Arthur G. Dove* (Berkeley, CA: The University of California Press, 1958), pp. 48, 38.

23 Barbara Haskell, *Arthur Dove* (Boston: New York Graphic Society, 1975), p. 33; Ann Lee Morgan, *Arthur Dove: Life and Work* (Newark, DE: University of Delaware Press, 1984), p. 78. For Dove's interest in theolosophy, see Sherrye Cohn, *Arthur Dove: Nature as Symbol* (Ann Arbor, MI: UMI Research Press, 1985).

Reforming the Image

torial hymns" which celebrate primary, mythic forces in nature. He links them to Vincent Van Gogh, Edvard Munch, and Emile Nolde, for whom the "sun becomes almost a holy icon."[24]

Is there an inherent, universal symbolism in nature? A common thread running through diverse interpretive frameworks is the use of nature as a principal iconographical source for religious knowledge and understanding. Clearly, as Rosenblum's study of northern Romantic artists shows, the choice of nature as a religious icon was not simply an American cultural phenomenon. When Calvin, Zwingli, and later the Puritans reformed liturgical spaces, emptying them of paintings and sculpture, they opened the way for artists themselves to develop non-ecclesiastical religious symbols. Many mystically inclined artists chose images of nature to reveal the mysterious connection between the physical and metaphysical and to witness to the presence of the infinite in the finite.

If nature is an occasion for religious revelation, does it mean then that all images of nature are filled with religious meaning? Or does the symbolic import depend upon the vision and faith of individual viewers? Or upon analogies derived from the study of other cultural forms? As we have seen, several nineteenth-century American artists, who clearly articulated religious concerns, found their inspiration in nature. Some modern historians have identified in other landscapists religious concerns that are implicit. At the same time, there are countless viewers who bring to *all* types of nature images—from Hudson River landscapes to Sierra Club calendars—a reverential and pious feeling for nature.

The freeing of the religious imagination from traditional icons permits artists *or* viewers to transform images of the ordi-

---

[24] Rosenblum, pp. 207, 133.

nary world into objects of meditation. Many artists have shown that commonplace objects of reality as well as natural forms can be envisioned as ablaze with spirit, witnessing to the presence and glory of God. This transformation from institutional, conventional symbols to personal ones means, however, that the arts become increasingly dependent upon a private, rather than corporate religious imagination. Seeking greater liberation, some artists later in the century abandoned even the abstract representations of nature, and indeed, turned away from all imagery of the phenomenal world. They looked inward in search of transcendent reality and their spiritual odysseys led them into the realm of non-representational art.

Redefining Religious Art

Although Arthur Dove and Georgia O'Keeffe were among the first artists to experiment with abstraction, their images, while simplified and distilled, were rooted in the world of natural forms. Dove remarked to Stieglitz, for example, that he had to keep returning to nature to keep his work vital. On the other hand, painters who wanted to sever all bonds with the phenomenal world and to develop a visual language for the embodiment of spirit sought a new language and content for their art. Unlike some nineteenth-century artists, they were not content with a spirit-filled vision of nature. A century after Durand, these visionary artists no longer found landscape, abstractly or realistically rendered, adequate for the expression of religious emotion. There had to be a radical break with styles and symbols of the past.

Two European artists, Wassily Kandinsky and Piet Mondrian, were deliberate and articulate about their aims to reform images and initiate new views of religious art. They stand out among their contemporaries because they wrote about their new concept of symbols and the communication of spirituality. At the same time, they created paintings which exemplified their theo-

Reforming the Image

ries. Their work and ideas would be sympathetically assimilated by a later generation of American abstract artists who became prominent in the 1940s and 50s.

Despite differences in style and conceptual framework, Kandinsky and Mondrian shared important convictions about the reform of images. One strong bond was their belief that abstract forms could become a universal visual language. They expected their revisions of western art to lead to commonly understood symbols which could transcend cultural barriers. Each was convinced that the new language of abstract art was destined for the communication of public—not simply personal—religious symbols. Mondrian, for example, asserted that the artist liberated from recognizable subjects is freer to "conquer individual expression and to reveal...the universal aspect of life."[25] The non-figurative language of abstract art represented for him the culmination of the long struggle of artists to communicate the "true image of reality." For his part, Kandinsky found in music an analogue for a basic, inherently intuitive form of visual communication. He believed that certain colors and shapes could communicate universal feelings and emotions. In his book *Concerning the Spiritual in Art*, Kandinsky described particular states of mind evoked by colors.[26]

Both artists, critical of the materialism which seemed to dominate western society, saw art as a means of spiritual reform. To Kandinsky, art possessed an "awakening prophetic power which

---

[25] Piet Mondrian, *Plastic Art and Pure Plastic Art, 1937, and Other Essays, 1941-1943* (New York: Wittenborn, Schultz, Inc., 1951), pp. 31, 39.

[26] Wassily Kandinsky, *Concerning the Spiritual in Art, and Painting in Particular 1912* (New York: George Wittenborn, 1947). See pages 54-66. For example, Kandinsky explains that green is the most restful color and lacks overtones of joy, grief, and passion. Yellow and blue, he says, actuate a sense of human participation in continuous cosmic motions.

can have far-reaching and profound effect." He was concerned that artists not distance themselves from social responsibility and he decried "art for art's sake," which was a popular idea among many artists of his time.[27] Similarly, Mondrian associated non-representational art with an evolution of social consciousness and was convinced that artists could open the way to a truer, less materialistic vision of reality.

Their critiques of western culture, as well as their language of abstract forms, emerged from a fundamental belief that art can reveal an absolute, metaphysical reality. Mondrian spoke of the function of art as a process of discovering the laws and principles of universal beauty: through art we evolve from subjective reality toward the "essence of things and of ourselves."[28] For Kandinsky as well, the aim of art is revelation. Form is the "*external expression of an inner meaning*," which can disclose and awaken the striving of the soul.[29] Both believed that artists are empowered to express and to share enduring truths. They were convinced that, as aesthetic mystics, artists understand spiritual reality more readily than most people and that their expressions evoke the life of the spirit.

To purify art of excessive subjectivity and to lead viewers to spiritual awareness, Kandinsky and Mondrian eliminated representational subject matter in their paintings. Kandinsky's early abstractions are composed of amorphous, dynamic shapes executed in bold, intense colors. While he wrote about the intrinsic meanings of circles, squares, triangles, and colors, his first non-representational works were more kaleidoscopic than geometric. These early abstract paintings showed his exuberant,

---

[27] *Ibid.*, p. 26.

[28] Mondrian, p. 51.

[29] Kandinsky, p. 47.

Reforming the Image

sensitive feeling for color and a confidence in its power to move
the spirit. Later, some shapes he used become more sharply de-
fined, while others appear biomorphic. Throughout his career,
however, the enduring article of faith for Kandinsky was the
conviction that non-representational forms do not direct the
viewer to the external world, but instead witness to an inner,
mystical world.

The elimination of representational elements led Mondrian
to a different type of aesthetic. His search for purity of form took
him through an exhaustive, systematic process of analyzing and
synthesizing basic visual components. Beginning with abstractions of trees, then dunes, and finally architectural structures,
Mondrian gradually eliminated all traces of iconographical
motifs and reduced his visual vocabulary to one of utmost simplicity. Eventually the painter worked only with vertical and
horizontal black lines and the primary colors, red, yellow, and
blue. His quest for the spiritual in art became an aesthetic *via
negativa*, a gradual stripping away of the familiar, recognizable
qualities of the palpable world. Mondrian's austere reduction of
the sensate was like the rigorous practices of the ascetic.
Through his purgation of visual experience he developed a modern aesthetic of emptiness in order to communicate an absolute
reality. Kandinsky and Mondrian initiated changes in the concept of religious art that moved far beyond conventional icons.
Working apart from liturgical contexts and ecclesiastical
themes, they hoped to create a vocabulary and syntax for the
expression of spirituality.[30]

Both artists were strongly influenced by theosophical and oc-
cult teachings, although Kandinsky retained his Orthodox faith

---

[30] E. A. Carmean, Jr., *Mondrian: The Diamond Compositions* (Washington, DC: The
National Gallery of Art, 1979), p. 42. Some interpreters of Mondrian have related his
diamond-shaped paintings to the escutcheons in Dutch church interiors.

throughout his life. Mondrian's theosophical ideas were tempered by Calvinist tradition.[31] From a variety of religious strands they sought to forge nothing less than a spiritual revolution through art, leading others to a universal metaphysical reality. In the face of materialism and the waning power of the church, these two artists saw a saving role for the arts in modern society, independent of the church's traditional icons and rituals, yet accessible to all.

A few American artists experimented with non-objective art early in the twentieth century, but Kandinsky and Mondrian had no widespread following. Indeed, when some Americans had their first glimpse of non-representational art at the famous Armory Show in New York City in 1913, there was general shock and outrage. The show was organized by a number of American artists who had traveled to Europe or had seen various types of *avant garde* art in small galleries. This exhibition was, for example, the initial exposure for many Americans to the non-objective color improvisations of Kandinsky; it also included the cubist, multifaceted figure studies of Marcel Duchamp. Many Americans, including influential persons like President Theodore Roosevelt, ridiculed these radical changes in visual representation. Except among artists, non-representational art was little understood and remained so for almost half a century. Then in the mid-twentieth century, abstract art entered a new phase, moving to center stage and into the limelight of the art world.

---

[31] See Michel Seuphor, *Piet Mondrian: Life and Work* (New York: Harry N. Abrams, 1956). Seuphor writes that Mondrian's Calvinism was strong, but tempered by a long and meticulous study of theosophy. Most commentators agree that both Kandinsky and Mondrian went beyond the dogmatic boundaries of the theosophical groups of their time. Sixen Ringbom, for example, finds theosophy the link which connects these artists to the tradition of formlessness in Eastern philosophy, as well as to the mystical tradition of Meister Eckhart, Johannes Tauler, Jacob Boehme, and others.

Reforming the Image

During the late 1940s and 50s, painters associated with the so-called New York School of abstract art gained national and international recognition in the post-war culture. In spite of the fact that these painters were just as difficult to understand as the early modern abstractionists, the public attitude had changed. Critics and mass media coverage quickly made them into celebrities.[32] Increasingly the "meaning" of abstract art was discussed, and opinions were circulated widely in magazines and newspapers; diverse critical interpretations and theories inevitably arose. Some critics brought in the concepts and vocabulary of psychoanalysis to decipher hidden meanings, while others stressed the political and revolutionary import. A few artists and interpreters continued to associate abstract art with religious symbolism. Three artists whose work has been viewed as the embodiment of spiritual experience are Barnett Newman, Mark Rothko, and Jackson Pollock. Unlike the pioneers of abstraction, however, they did not develop theories or leave extensive written documents; consequently, art critics have played an essential role in identifying and explaining the religious symbolism in their paintings.

Barnett Newman's late paintings were characterized by the simplicity of shapes and intensity of color, but even so, he gave them titles that often included cosmological, mystical, or biblical references. In 1948, for example, he painted *Onement One* using rich but sparse colors. A dark, brownish red defines the ground of a rectangular canvas which is divided evenly by a thin dark strip and overpainted with a loosely brushed bright orange.

---

[32] James Ackerman, "The Demise of the Avant Garde," *L'Arte* 6 (1969): 4-11. Historian James Ackerman has pointed out that American society itself had altered considerably and become accustomed to change and novelty. It was less fixed in its traditions, less apt to be "disturbed and offended by works of art that abandoned accepted standards in search for new form and meaning." At the same time, he noted, the radical artist found widespread acceptance more readily than the conservative.

Standing before this large painting one experiences its compelling austerity and the impact of pure shapes and colors. Many
viewers feel no need to transpose inarticulate reactions into
words, but critics have attempted to explain Newman's symbolism in the light of his life, religious interests, and artistic
development.

For Thomas Hess, *Onement One* is a celebration of the act of
creation: "a complex symbol, in the purest sense, of Genesis itself." It symbolizes God's primal gesture, starting with the void
and creating light from darkness.[33] Hess relates this and other
paintings to Newman's interest in Jewish mysticism and compares him to the mystics of the Kabbalah who sought the hidden
God in silence and privacy.

Critic Harold Rosenberg, also aware of the artist's religious
interests, asserts that Newman could no longer conceive of a
visual narration of biblical themes and therefore had to paint
the *idea* of them. Viewers were invited to participate in the
sacred stories through the abstractions constructed by the artist.
At the same time, however, Rosenberg is skeptical about the
capacity of such abstractions to convey particular religious
themes. Even an artist's explicit interest in spirituality does not,
he says, assure communication through non-representational
forms. The religious interpretations of paintings by appreciative
critics do not "settle the problem of what the rectangles and zips
mean." Newman's painting, he concludes, was the artist's way of
"practicing the sublime, not of conveying it."[34]

Paintings by Mark Rothko have also been regarded as objects
of great spiritual power and expressiveness. Like Newman, he

---

[33] Thomas B. Hess, *Barnett Newman* (New York: The Museum of Modern Art, 1971),
p. 56.

[34] Harold Rosenberg, "Meaning in Abstract Art" in *New Yorker*, January 1, 1972,
p. 46.

Reforming the Image

believed that he was abandoning the use of familiar objects and subject matter for the sake of expressing a mythic reality which could no longer be communicated through conventional symbols. Statements by Rothko have assisted critics in their religious interpretations of his paintings. For example, he remarked to an interviewer that he was not an abstractionist in the sense of being preoccupied simply with form and color relationships. Stressing his singular concern for basic human experiences and emotions, "tragedy, ecstasy, doom," Rothko pointed out that some people break down and cry in front of his paintings. This, he said, indicated that he was communicating at a profound level: "The people who weep before my pictures are having the same religious experience I had when I painted them, and if you say you are moved only by these color relationships, then you miss the point."[35] Unlike Newman, Rothko made no literary references in his titles to the basic experiences he was expressing. The titles are, rather, generally descriptive of the formal elements in his paintings, for example, *Four Darks in Red* or *Blue, Green, and Brown.*

Rothko consciously looked upon himself as one of a small number of mythmakers. Art historian Anna Chave has meticulously detailed the artist's development, following his persistent interest in myth and his continuous search for images that would have universal significance. Present throughout various phases of his work—from surrealist motifs to the large, sombre paintings done late in his life—was Rothko's enduring aim to evoke in viewers a sense of the mystery of the human condition. "Rothko believed he needed myth to portray the inner self," Chave writes, "because he had a vision of mythology as encom-

---

[35] Seldon Rodman, *Conversations with Artists* (New York: Devin-Adair, 1957), p. 93.

passing the essence of human psychology and emotion."[36] Myths could offer artists eternal symbols of human feelings and experience. Yet his search for meaningful forms led Rothko eventually to the expansive rectangular paintings with carefullly measured layers of color that draw viewers into their contemplative space. These late non-representational works presented no narrative structure, no sacred or heroic dramas. Instead they summon serious viewers into a color-filled silence. Because the artist himself experienced a fundamental tension between belief and unbelief, Chave compares Rothko with Abraham and Kierkegaard. But, she says, unlike them, "it seems that he could not conclusively make up his mind to believe." [37]Thus critics may have opposite responses to his paintings. For some, a Rothko painting may fail to confirm or deny faith, while others find in them a power ascribed to icons, to inspire and nurture religious reflection.

In their reformulation of religious art, Kandinsky and Mondrian had concentrated on the spiritual symbolism of non-representational art. Similarly the paintings of Newman and Rothko were expected to evoke contemplation in the viewers even though they, too, were not placed in a liturgical setting. To some artists, however, the making of a painting—the direct experience with pigment on the canvas—often took on overtones of ritual action. In the 1950s a number of abstract artists began to place special importance on the physical activity of creating a work, which suggests a new and different religious dimension. As in ritual, the creation of a work of art can provide an opportunity to lose oneself in a larger whole, dissolving the boundaries of consciousness normally experienced by the ego.

---

[36] Anna Chave, *Mark Rothko: Subjects in Abstraction* (New Haven, CT: Yale University Press, 1989), p. 91.

[37] *Ibid.*, p. 197.

Reforming the Image

Traditional religious ritual allows believers to withdraw from ordinary reality, to experience a sense of renewal, and then return to everyday life with assurance and hope. By comparison, some painters might find the total engagement with paint and canvas an occasion for withdrawal and transformation.

Harold Rosenberg finds an analogy between traditional tribal ritual action and the making of an art object. He identifies Jackson Pollock as a painter whose will to make a painting and the ensuing physical activity were central to the creative process. Pollock, is, he wrote, an artist who has a secret, the secret of magic; he is a peer of Navajo sand painters. His art, like theirs, is ritualistic. Rosenberg emphasizes, however, the solitary action of the individual artist:

> For this "sand painter," the painting was medicine for the artist himself, not for a patient brought out of his tent to be cured for a fee of two goats. Contact was Pollock's salvation, and he tried to make it appear afresh in each painting.[38]

While similarities to ritual are found, especially in action painting, this analogy also exposes profound differences. In traditional religious settings images and objects generally accompanied communal religious experiences; in the later twentieth century, however, artists have tended to explore personal symbols and enact private rituals. Increasingly artists, interpreters, and viewers have come to associate the practice of high art with an individual search for salvation.

Art: An Individual Spiritual Odyssey

Diverse speculation about the meaning of abstract art, widely publicized in the 1950s, has weakened the idea that it displays

---

[38] Harold Rosenberg, "The Mythic Act," in *Artworks and Packages* (New York: Dell, 1971), p. 68.

universal religious symbolism. Yet while critics disagreed among themselves about the interpretation of these images, many at the time believed that artists were destined to explore the boundaries of human experience, delving into the innermost recesses of spirit and psyche. Artists, set apart from ordinary individuals, were notable not for creating public symbols, but for exploring personal visions and emotions.

In the post-war climate of existentialism certain theologians helped to shape perceptions of the heroic, even the saving, nature of the creative act. At a time when few Protestant theologians demonstrated an explicit concern for the arts, Paul Tillich brought them to the forefront of his theological analysis of culture. He became a central figure in accentuating the artist's individual spiritual quest, and while he was especially interested in Expressionism, his theological views lent force to the religious interpretation of artistic activity in general.

Tillich provided the interpreters of art with a theological basis for attributing religious significance to non-ecclesiastical painting and sculpture. He maintained, for example, that biblical or mythical subjects did not assure genuine religious art, and, he was, in fact, critical of the highly sentimental portrayals found in much official church art. Tillich characterized Hoffman's representation of Jesus at Riverside Church in New York City as sentimental and compared it with others that portray Jesus as a "rheumatic or otherwise sick, dull school teacher walking through little villages."[39] Mediocre art could not, in Tillich's view, move the spirit. At the same time, he contended that non-ecclesiastical art, regardless of subject matter, could have a religious dimension.

---

[39] Paul Tillich, "Existentialist Aspects of Modern Art" in *Christianity and the Existentialists* (New York: Charles Scribner's Sons, 1956), p. 139.

Reforming the Image

Releasing religious art from the confines of liturgical settings and themes, Tillich stated that *any* subject could become a revelatory event, an occasion to fathom the depths of reality. In the hands of a sensitive artist, an ordinary subject—still life, landscape, portrait, genre, or abstraction—could communicate an ultimate concern for being. In formulating his theology of art, Tillich built upon what he called the fundamental Protestant principle—"God is present in secular existence as much as he is present in sacred existence." To illustrate this he recalled his attraction to a seventeenth-century Dutch painting, an interior scene with "play, dance, drunkenness, love, and everything together." Tillich asked himself what the picture expressed in terms of human existence and then answered that it spoke of an affirmation of life, an unrestricted vitality that was almost ecstatic. In such a painting the "power of being is visible, not directly, but indirectly," and this type of communication Tillich called "indirectly religious."[40]

While Tillich's "Protestant principle" permitted all subjects to be potential sources of revelation, he was more exclusive when it came to religious styles and attributed particular spiritual significance to Expressionism. In that style he discerned a unique power to convey the depths of human experience. The expressionistic artist looks into the abyss of reality, below the surface of appearance and organic unity, forsaking the beauty of impressionism and idealism. Natural forms are disrupted and distorted; yet embodied in such inorganic forms is "the power of being itself." In this category Tillich placed artists like Vincent Van Gogh, Edvard Munch, and Pablo Picasso. He saw in Van Gogh's *Night Cafe*, for example, the "horror of emptiness," while of Picasso's *Guernica* he wrote that in this work one sees "the

---

[40] *Ibid.*, pp. 134, 135.

human situation without any cover." Picasso's painting expressed the unthinkable—the bombing in 1936 of the small Spanish town by Italian and German planes, the first experience of the killing of civilians in an air raid. Tillich explained that it could also show what is in the souls of Americans and others, "the disruptiveness, existential doubt, emptiness, and meaninglessness." From Tillich's perspective, the Protestant legacy compels the artist to look at human estrangement and despair—not to cover up reality, but to disclose and explore its depths.[41]

Tillich's existential vision reinforced a view of art as witness to a solitary, spiritual journey. He was especially appreciative of artists whose work reflected their experiences with anxiety and despair. In his book *Courage to Be*, the theologian describes the creative process as heroic. Confronted by the abyss of life's meaninglessness, an artist faces and expresses it. Tillich would have understood and appreciated the view of art expressed by Rothko and some of his colleagues: "To us art is an adventure into an unknown world which can be explored only by those willing to take risks."[42] To Tillich, even though a painting conveys a sense of void and meaninglessness, that in itself can be a confirmation rather than a denial of being. The *act* of making images and objects, whatever their content, enables the artist to transcend human suffering. In *Theology of Culture*, Tillich characteristically wrote: "He who can bear and express meaninglessness shows that he experiences meaning within his desert of meaninglessness."[43]

---

[41] *Ibid.*, pp. 136, 138.

[42] Chave, pp. 80, 207 (n. 39).

[43] Paul Tillich, *Theology of Culture* (New York: Oxford University Press, 1964), p. 75.

Reforming the Image

Like other existentialists, he attributed a saving dimension to the creative process itself. These views were particularly applicable to certain types of non-representational art. Action painting, abstractions violently executed and thickly layered with pigment, could dramatically document the ritualistic soul-searching of the artist. Placed in a museum, such paintings could evoke reverent responses from a respectful public. Religiously inclined and sympathetic viewers could meditate on the dark night of the soul and the artist's quest for meaning.

Tillich's theology of art gave Protestants new ways of thinking about the religious functions of visual images. Although he valued the traditional use of art in churches, the theologian was disturbed that the old symbols spoke to only a few people. And, of course, he was especially concerned with the religious dimensions of secular culture. In his view, a genuinely prophetic and meditative art that exists outside of liturgical space needs to be recognized. His thought was welcomed by Protestants who appreciated the visual arts, but resisted their use in churches. Tillich formulated a justification for art that was "religious" without limiting it to places of worship. Those uneasy with paintings and sculpture in the sanctuary could follow in the museum the spiritual journeys of prophets, seers, and mystics.

From another perspective, philosopher Susanne Langer was, like Tillich, interested in the arts' expressive power, and she called attention to the importance of an individual artist's feelings. She did so by distinguishing two types of symbolization in a work of art. First, she identified what she called the "symbol in art" which communicates shared, commonly understood meanings and refers to something beyond itself—myths, sacred texts, significant historical episodes. In this category are found not only traditional biblical narratives and Greek mythologies, but also the modern human experiences represented in Picasso's *Guernica*. The "symbol in art" provides an objective reference beyond the artist or viewers, yet one to which they can relate their own experiences.

In contrast to this familiar concept of symbol, she describes a second type, the "art symbol" which, she says, has been neglected or missed entirely. This is a more primitive function of symbolization which articulates the life of feeling, the dynamic flux of personal existence. We encounter the art symbol through what meets the eye. It does not stand for something else, nor does it refer to anything that exists apart from it. Through colors, forms, and textures of a painting, for example, viewers apprehend the private, innermost being of the artist. What we take in through our eyes is the "appearance of feeling," the character of the inner life, which only the sensuous or poetic form can voice. The art symbol, she wrote, is the absolute image, "the image of what would otherwise be irrational." The untranslatable physicality of the painting—hue, brushstrokes, light—directly present us with emotion, vitality, personal identity—life lived and felt.[44]

As a philospher, Langer seems to put into words many of the expectations and hopes of abstract expressionists such as Newman, Rothko, and Pollock. Only in the physical presence of a work can "meaning" be experienced. The materiality of the painting itself is the sole access to the feelings of the artist. In their abstractions there are no familiar signs to lead obliquely to the painter's inner being and emotions. That can only be known through color, texture, line, scale, light, and brush stroke. Today, in an age of lavish, ubiquitous color reproductions, the idea of communication only through the physical involvement with a painting may have been lost. A reproduction—no matter how accurate—precludes the kind of

---

[44] Susanne K. Langer, "The Art Symbol and the Symbol in Art" in *Problems of Art: Ten Philosophical Lectures* (New York: Charles Scribner's Sons, 1957), pp. 127, 132-139.

Reforming the Image

engagement with viewers that abstract expressionists sought. From their perspective, only through the immediate encounter with a work can there be a sacramental experience in which the invisible becomes visible.

The originators of twentieth-century abstract painting, Kandinsky and Mondrian, had envisioned it as a unifying symbolic force, an expression of spirituality that transcended doctrine and culture. By mid-century American artists and critics had transformed non-representational art into the visual poetry of individual spiritual journeys. Although their viewpoints arose from different disciplines, both Tillich and Langer underscored the significance of the interior life of individual artists and the experiential dramas which occur there. As an expression of the artist's feeling or spiritual wanderings, abstract art is remarkably suitable. Without the distractions of visual metaphors, pure pigments and forms narrow and intensify our engagement. Paintings become embodiments of feeling.

While a number of abstract painters expressed interest in spirituality, relatively few have created works of art for a place of worship. Mark Rothko is a notable exception. Between 1964 and 1967, he executed a series of paintings which are now located in an interdenominational chapel at Rice University in Houston, Texas. In the ritual space at Houston, the large, somber triptychs and panels surround viewers and draw them into the rich voids of black and deep maroon. There are no conventional symbols associated with particular traditions. The only iconic references have to be deduced from the shape of the space and the measured series of fourteen paintings usually associated with the Stations of the Cross. These are grouped into three triptychs and five single panels. Darker and more foreboding than Rothko's earlier canvases, they dominate the walls and frame the octagonal chapel. Toward the end of his life the painter was thoroughly absorbed in the work for this sacred space.

Yet the nature of faith expressed in these works remains mysterious. Perhaps the paintings reveal the abyss to which Tillich referred, where meaning is found in the desert of meaninglessness. Despite their dark tonality, however, these paintings create a liturgical atmosphere comparable to that developed by the Cistercians. This chapel manifests an aesthetic of emptiness, and like those earlier religious spaces, it derives power from the aniconic aesthetic: carefully constructed geometric, abstract shapes, contrasts of darkness and lightness, and concern for order and measure. Moreover, in the Houston chapel, as in St. Bernard's churches, the imageless aesthetic is enlivened and enriched through the iconography and drama of rituals that take place there. Within this meditative environment, particular religious symbols are introduced by denominational rites and ceremonies. In this setting the spiritual quests of religious groups and that of the artist are joined.

From Icon to Commodity

The icons and rituals of most contemporary artists are more private than public, and the authenticity of their symbols rests in individual, not community experience. While the art activity may be redemptive for the artist, the high arts are no longer expected to convey commonly understood and accepted values and meanings. Indeed, in today's marketplace, the arts' novelty and lack of meaning contribute to their value as a special commodity. For a secular technological society, esoteric meanings enhance the mystique of "art," which has taken on a sacred aura and is treasured in the same way that other societies have prized relics and trophies. Tom Wolfe argues that "art" itself, whatever the medium or style, is now accorded the reverence befitting a

Reforming the Image

deity. With characteristic irreverence toward the art establishment, he comments: "Today the conventional symbol of devoutness is—but of course—the Holy Rectangle: the painting."[45] Paintings and sculptures are the holy objects which adorn the offices and plazas of corporate headquarters and homes of the wealthy.

The sacralization of art goes hand in hand with its importance as a commodity; images and objects are valued more for their commercial worth and prestige than for the symbolization of shared meanings. Supplanting form, function, and meaning, money has become the essential metaphor. Robert Hughes, critic and commentator on contemporary culture, in his article, "Art and Money,"[46] has documented changing attitudes about the worth of art which have occurred over the last two or three hundred years. He is careful, however, not to romanticize the starving artist and prefaces his remarks by noting that connections between patronage, money, and trade have been around for a long time. Money does not, he says, necessarily corrupt the artistic imagination. At the same time, however, Hughes shows how twentieth-century art has increasingly been viewed like stocks, bonds, and gold; it can be expected to rise in monetary value with the passage of time and especially with the passing of the artist. We have become accustomed to thinking of works of art as investment commodities. Hughes points out that the greatest shifts toward the merchandising of art occurred after 1960, and he attributes this to the great liquidity of late twentieth-century wealth. The art market successfully convinced affluent individuals that, while the arts don't bear interest, they

---

[45] Tom Wolfe, "The Worship of Art: Notes on the New God" in *Harper's* (October, 1984), p. 63.

[46] Robert Hughes, "On Art and Money," *The New York Review of Books* 31:19 (1984), pp. 20-27.

offer dramatic and consistent capital gains, as well as the more intangible pleasures of ownership. While Hughes centers on the changing relationships between art and money, his views parallel those of other critics concerned with social functions of art and the values presently ascribed to it.

Women artists and critics were among the first to challenge the entrepreneurial attitudes of dealers and galleries and to protest the dislocation of art from its humanistic base in communal experience. During the 1960s and 70s feminists sought to reclaim traditional social roles of the visual arts and at the same time to overturn aesthetic conventions and theories that led to insularity and overvaluation as a commodity. While the range of interests among contemporary women artists has become quite extensive, there are certain themes which are significant to the continuing reformulation of religious art.

Lucy Lippard, for example, has been an articulate feminist voice for a more inclusive, socially responsible function of the visual arts in today's world. Critical of the heroic individualism associated with many twentieth-century painters and sculptors, she has drawn attention to the vital sources of art in commonly held world views and myths of earlier religious cultures. While there may no longer be any one unified symbol system for a complex pluralistic world, she continues to emphasize the essential role of the arts in communicating human meanings and values. Moreover, Lippard and other feminists have pointed out the nurturing, reconciling role that the arts may play. Women artists in particular, says Lippard are able to "reach out and integrate art and life, idea and sensation—or nature and culture."[47]

In exploring the social dimensions of the arts, women have frequently turned to non-western or prehistoric religions in

---

[47] Lucy Lippard, *Overlay: Contemporary Art and the Art of Prehistory* (New York: Pantheon, 1983), p. 42.

Reforming the Image

which female symbolization was paramount or equally important to that of the male in representing the cosmic scheme of
things. There also the unknown mysteries of the natural and supernatural world are symbolized in concrete, commonly understood experiences of sexuality, birth, nurture, and death. Similarly women artists today draw us deeper into matter, replacing
cerebral, disembodied metaphysics with palpable human metaphors for life's truths and mysteries. Women sculptors—such as
Nancy Holt and Alice Aycock—in their work on sites have
brought new perspectives to age-old relationships with nature.
These and other women artists take their place alongside revolutionary feminist theologians who point out that those who
have long pretended to speak for the human condition and our
experience of God have been men. In different ways both
women artists and thinkers are, observes theologian Sallie
McFague, claiming that "the experience of half the human race
has not been acknowledged by the Judaic-Christian tradition."[48]

In drawing "art" back into life, feminists have experimented
with materials, processes, and spaces different from those of the
mid-century mythmakers. Judy Pfaff, for example, has moved
from large expressionistic paintings into three-dimensional in-
stallations, using all kinds of materials, many of which are im-
permanent and untypical of high art—fabrics, paper, copper
wire, neon, and Day-Glo colors. Working on site to create a
total environment, she has transformed the two-dimensional
ritualism of a Pollock painting into a playful, walk-in ritual
world for others.

From another perspective, art historian James Ackerman has
underscored the need for contemporary artists to address the
function of art and its responsibility for the communication not

---

[48] Sallie McFague, *Metaphorical Theology: Models of God in Religious Language*
(Philadelphia: Fortress Press, 1982), p. 154.

of private symbols, but of social values and meanings. Following the widespread acceptance of the abstractionists of the 1950s, the public has come to expect novelty in the communication of private realities. "We have made art," he argues, "into a functionless luxury, subject to manipulation in the marketplace in the same way as fashionable clothing." The museum has become an artificial environment, and the visual arts increasingly removed from a living culture. To fulfill their age-old function of embodying social values, they must move again into the public domain, recovering a role both communal and communicative. "I expect the greatest art," Ackerman says, "both to address us in our private realms and to lead us to intensified perceptions of shared (or shareable) experience."[49]

Throughout the 1980s, however, artists and collectors have been caught up in the metamorphosis of art objects into commodities for a consumer society. Ironically, works that manifest a search for religious meaning or reflect social values are themselves scooped up like spiritual "droppings," publicized, and marketed to the highest bidder. Yet this speculative approach to art has been accompanied by cynicism and a certain malaise. The 1980s also brought a tedious recycling of styles and an endless proliferation of "isms" and "neo-isms."

Are there any alternatives for artists who want their work to perform a larger social and sacramental role? Or will "art" continue to be exclusively for artists and those in society who can afford the luxury of collecting? Philosopher-critic Arthur Danto suggests that we may now be approaching the end of art as we have understood it during the modern era. He cites, for example, the trauma that beset painting with the advent of photo-

---

[49] James S. Ackerman, "Judgments of Value," in *Studies in Art History: Presented at the Middle Atlantic Symposium in the History of Art 1971-73* (College Park, MD: University of Maryland, 1973), pp. 34, 35.

graphy and film. During the twentieth century, Danto claims, art has become essentially preoccupied with its own self-identity. Andy Warhol's Brillo boxes exhibited in museums boldly challenged the very nature of art. As artists became increasingly preoccupied with the question, "What is Art?" they moved steadily toward philosophy. Finally, Danto says, art has become " vaporized in a *dazzle* of pure thought about itself," and remains solely the object of its theoretical consciousness.[50] In saying that we have reached the end of art does not, from Danto's perspective, mean that there will be no image or object-making. On the contrary, the visual arts may be freed from self-consciousness to serve and enhance human experience in a variety of ways.

Danto's ideas may be especially liberating for those who care about art but have been impatient with the solipsism which has settled in. Makers of images and objects in various disciplines—sculptors, photographers, printmakers, weavers, painters, ceramicists—all who wish to be, may be free from the presumption of identifying the nature of art. Danto's refreshing idea of the "end of art" may indeed signal a new beginning, one which encourages many different questions to be raised simultaneously. For some it may be one of seeking places where art may function in a social context, a chance for it to be once again "wrapped up in life...desired not for its own sake, but to decorate life with the splendor which it could bestow."[51] Other artists will want to continue with the question "What is art?" and move even deeper into philosophy. Those interested in the continuing reformulation of religious art may ask: What are the meaningful symbols shared today? How and where may these be expressed?

---

[50] Arthur C. Danto, *The Philosophical Disenfranchisement of Art* (New York: Columbia University Press, 1986), p. 111.

[51] Huizinga, p. 244.

Corporate Religious Symbols

Historically, traditional subjects selected by church leaders were consistent sources of religious symbolism. Painters and sculptors were not responsible for inventing sacred iconography. "Invention" in the arts meant, in fact, a new, fresh vision of old, time-worn subjects familiar to everyone. Through the aesthetic imagination the artists transformed and revitalized established themes. Thus nativity scenes by Giotto and El Greco differ enormously, each a unique rendering of a familiar subject. While compositional elements—color, line, texture, and space—might be modified by the faith, talents and historical contexts of individual artists, the subjects reflected corporate, shared religious knowledge. Even though the belief systems in which they arose has been called into question, the paintings themselves continue to witness to particular myths. Today, those who stand outside the Christian world view may miss some levels of meaning and complexity in an altarpiece. Nevertheless, the conventional symbols—sometimes only dimly perceived—still bear the burden of religious communication.

Whatever their style, the shared meanings and functions of traditional religious icons were confirmed by their presence in liturgical space. The earliest forms of Christian art—at Dura-Europos and the catacombs—arose from the visual language of late classical imagery, adapted for particular rites and ceremonies, baptism and burial. The arts were not conceived simply as the individual expression of the artist, but were part of a total, corporate enactment of faith. While later there were individual artists, artisans, or schools that became distinguished for style and consummate craftsmanship, the purpose of the works themselves was to enhance liturgy. Johann Huizinga points out in *The Waning of the Middle Ages* that the great art of this period can be seen essentially as an "applied art," a term that may offend artists who claim autonomy for art.

Reforming the Image

When the sixteenth-century reformers removed the visual arts from the churches, some religiously inclined artists, especially those in Protestant countries, sought meaningful icons outside of traditional institutions. In this chapter I have used a number of American artists to trace the movement of the visual arts from within the church out into the mainstream of secular culture. Where the Protestant ethos dominated in nineteenth-century America the liturgical role of religious art remained largely unfulfilled. Moreover, except for a few patrons, there was little interest in biblical or allegorical subjects, as Thomas Cole discerned in his vain attempt to win an audience for religious and didactic subjects. Instead, landscape emerged as a subject that was popular and could be inspirational on many levels. For philosophers like Emerson and Coleridge, being in the presence of nature was a sacramental occasion, for there God was revealed. To painters like Durand and Inness landscape painting became an icon, a form for mediating this religious truth.

Yet in the absence of any specific theological interest, the attribution of religious meaning to landscape became problematic. Increasingly the evidence for spiritual symbolism moved away from the art object, and the meanings had to be supported by the subjective, revelatory claims of individuals—artists, critics, historians, and viewers.

In the twentieth century the pioneers of abstract art—Kandinsky and Mondrian—claimed a special role for non-representational art; to them it was a universal language for the communication of spiritual reality. In a few decades, however, this unified vision gave way to meditative individualized expression. In mid-century America religiously sensitive painters such as Newman and Rothko used abstraction as a means of exploring the life of the spirit. Without institutional patronage, however, artists with metaphysical interests became isolated seers or mystics. Only a few produced works for traditional religious communities.

Instead the appropriate space for contemplation seemed to be the museum, not the sanctuary. As Tillich observed, the artist's exploration of the problem of meaning became itself a courageous affirmation of being. Meditative art was no longer limited to spaces for worship. Artists today who continue to explore the life of the spirit personify the vision of nineteenth-century painter Washington Allston of the artist as a prophet or seer in the community. Their icons, however, often derive from a personal vocabulary of myths and symbols. In defense of these, they point to the shallow understanding of the arts among congregations and to the sentimentality of much official religious art. It is a dilemma not easily solved.

Late in the twentieth century, even as it takes its place alongside stocks and bonds as an investment commodity, art has increasingly assumed a religious mystique. Museums, like massive, walk-through reliquaries, are filled with awesome but rootless objects, far removed from real human community, where visual symbols of a different kind define both individual and communal meanings.

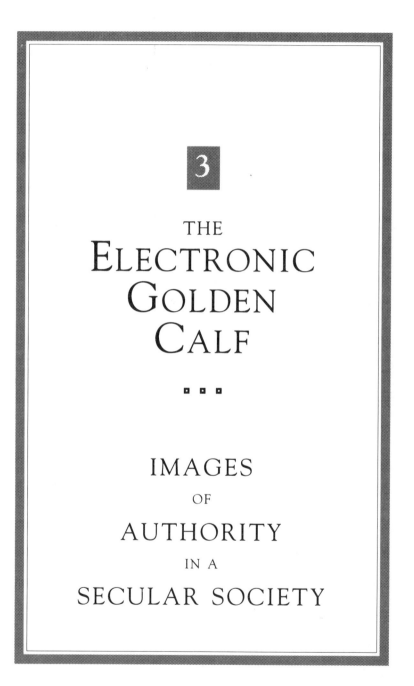

3

THE
ELECTRONIC GOLDEN CALF

■ ■ ■

IMAGES
OF
AUTHORITY
IN A
SECULAR SOCIETY

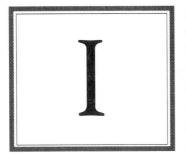

n their gradual disengagment from shared symbols, artists have left a vacuum. The public communication of myths, a responsibility and power assumed by high art in earlier centuries, has during the twentieth century been taken over by the images of popular culture. As we have observed, twentieth-century painters and sculptors turned inward to explore individual feelings and to express private visions. By contrast, American popular culture has followed a different course, inheriting roles once played by the high arts. The representation of social realities, traditionally delegated by state and ecclesiastical authorities to the visual arts, has migrated to the realm of the mass media, especially television.

Contemporary American culture is saturated with electronic images—the Super Bowl, the 700 Club, the funeral of a national leader, the nightly news programs, soap operas, countless commercials. These put us in touch with events—real and imaginary—and attune us to values beyond our immediate experience of time and space. More than simply pictures, the images mediate realities that are otherwise inaccessible to us and, at the same time, communicate a sense of what is important. Moreover, like images we looked at earlier, they perform a sacramental function; through them we not only "take part" in communal activities but are also indoctrinated with attitudes and points of view.

My primary concern is not the aesthetics of the media but the process by which fundamental social, political, and economic values are mediated to the public. We shall observe how television in particular performs sacramental functions in contemporary American culture. Traditionally sacramental images have rendered visible invisible religious truths, and in a

The Electronic Golden Calf

secular society as well, images can give concrete, vivid embodiment to some of the intangible beliefs of a culture. Conceived in
a larger framework, which includes all areas of human experience, such images tend to provide a basis for knowledge and
action.

This mediation of norms, authority, and information Bryan
Wilson has called the *latent* function of religion, in contrast to
its manifest role of salvation. Contemporary societies, he writes,
may operate with little recourse to religion as a social institu-
tion. "If modern states are largely secular in operation, this is
because the social arrangements of [human beings] are now no
longer dependent on the latent functions of religion."[1] What
this means is that we no longer look to the church or synagogue
for interpretations of all spheres of human activity. Instead, information and explanations of "how things are" are fragmented
and diversified, spread throughout cultural agencies. Today
science, government, technology, business, labor, education,
and the arts are all autonomous, free from the dictates of religion.

By contrast, ancient and medieval religions played a role in
personal salvation, giving at the same time coherence and order
to the surrounding culture. Traditional religious images symbolized this synthesis. At the church of St. Mary Madeleine, in
Vézelay, for example, the activities of the ordinary world—the
planting, harvesting, celebrating, and the movement of the seasons—radiated from the christological drama, which integrated
the natural and supernatural orders. Today no such all-embrac-
ing, unified vision exists, but even in a secular society, symbolic
representations of our collective life reinforce certain kinds of

---

[1] Bryan Wilson, *Religion in Sociological Perspective* (New York: Oxford University Press, 1982), p. 45. See Chapter 2, "The Functions of Religion in Contemporary Society.".

beliefs and values. We can expect to find these symbols now in the massive array of public images which technology has made possible. Television is a prime source of such sacramental images. If we look closely at different kinds of programs, we discern residual elements of traditional imperial and religious symbols of authority—mythic, informational, political.

First, American values are personified in heroes and heroines of sit-coms, dramas, soap operas and commercials. Like ancient myths and medieval legends, these popular forms tell easily understood stories of love and hate, birth and death, success and failure, loyalty and betrayal. Second, nightly news programs map the cosmos with images that define for us the contours of reality. News commentators, like ancient priests, lead us through ceremonies that purport to represent and explain worldwide events. Third, coverage of our political leaders has created authoritative images comparable to the statuary of the ancient world; television's "photo opportunities" have taken the place of sculpted portraits of rulers like Pericles and Caesar Augustus.

Mythic Authority: Tales of the Good Life

Several critics of the media have adapted the concept of "myth," using its anthropological and sociological meanings to shed light on the broader functions of television in American culture. British media critic Roger Silverstone suggests that television mythology expresses "a need and a constraint."[2] Even secular societies depend upon stories to communicate shared meanings and to set limits to what is socially acceptable. As Homeric myths identified common loyalties and set boundaries for the Hellenes, so popular art forms today witness to collective world views and portray current heroes and anti-heroes.

---

[2] Roger Silverstone, "Mass Communication Relies on Narrative and Myth," *Media Development*, 34/2 (1987):2

The Electronic Golden Calf

Television tells stories which are readily identifiable and offer reassurance; they provide "something of the elementary, the primary, the fundamental and stable." Without some commonly accepted narratives that articulate the truths and falsehoods, the values and disvaluations of a culture, we would find life intolerably disorienting. In this sense television's "entertainment" programs may speak to a human need for identity, both individual and social. As to the constraints of popular mythology, Silverstone points out that the mythic "worlds" that television constructs within the real world may operate in a conservative and restraining way—politically, socially, and economically. Conflicts and resolutions narrated in the popular mythology of television tend to reinforce existing institutions. While traditional myths and rituals provided some opportunities for identifiable change, the modifications of contemporary values and institutions brought about through television are less clear.[3] One cannot measure the actual effects of television upon viewers, nor can one ever be sure what people make of the things they hear and see. Still it is important to analyze the medium's narratives and symbols.

Looking at current offerings on prime-time television in the United States, we find it difficult to disagree with Todd Gitlin's claim that with few exceptions its heroes and heroines are preoccupied with self-interest. "If not utterly consumed by ambition and the fear of ending up as losers, these characters take both ambition and the fear for granted."[4] Glamorous incarnations of desire, they long only for private happiness. There is little concern for public good, and they seem content with the existing institutional order. The familiar images that open the

---

[3] Ibid., pp. 2-3.

[4] Todd Gitlin, *Inside Prime Time* (New York: Pantheon Books, 1985), p. 268.

program *Dallas* set the stage for the characters' persistent drive for money and control: the cityscape with its skyline of corporate headquarters, the stately ranch compound of the Ewing family, oil rigs silhouetted against the horizon, and heroic images of cowboys rounding up a massive herd of cattle. In their various roles as businessmen, worldwide oil speculators, and ranchers, the Ewing brothers, as well as their adversaries, constantly struggle to acquire and to dominate. Only in his role of father does J.R. seem to soften and momentarily modify his preoccupation with success and power.

One can, nevertheless, point to a few shows whose mythological characters are less avaricious and solipsistic. They combine stories and pictures depicting America as a special place where dreams are fulfilled and the liberty of all people assured. *The Cosby Show*, for example, has been one of the highest rated programs over the last several years. The episodes narrate the activities of an upper-middle-class black family. The head of the Huxtable household is a doctor. Sharing familial authority is his wife, also a professional person—a lawyer. Their home is located in a mixed, urban neighborhood. As individual family members enter into neighborhood and professional life, viewers are drawn into broader issues and social concerns.

One episode, for example, included the older generation, the parents of the couple. The story focused on the efforts of Theo, the teenage son, to write an essay on Martin Luther King, Jr. His firsts attempts were seen to lack, at least to the parents and grandparents, a real understanding of the magnitude of King's leadership and of the civil rights struggle. This led the grandparents to reflect on the momentous occasions of the 1960s—the demonstrations at lunch counters and the bus rides in which many black people risked their lives. Their recollections were somber and moving. They led the family in singing the familiar songs that had encouraged heroism and strengthened their faith during turbulent moments.

The Electronic Golden Calf

Not all episodes deal explicitly with racial issues. Generally, themes center on the basic human concerns of middle-class families, cutting across social and ethnic divisions. For example, the Huxtables want their children to excel in school and marry well. They are choosy about whom their children date and are especially critical of their daughters' suitors. In one episode, the Huxtables are shocked by the married daughter and son-in-law, Sondra and Alvin, who announce that they plan to open a "wilderness store" in Brooklyn rather than carry on their professional studies in law and medicine. Other small vignettes show the changing expectations in a marriage when both partners have important, productive careers. For example, Cliff Huxtable is depicted puttering around the kitchen as often as his wife; Clair Huxtable shares in making important decisions. Moreover, her professional commitments mean that Cliff has to assume a large share of the children's upbringing. There are many touching scenes between the father and his children: advising Vanessa, playing basketball with Theo, and teaching the youngest daughter, Rudy, how to ride her bicycle.

Especially symbolic is the home itself. Most of *The Cosby Show* takes place within the comfortable Huxtable home; the settings make strong visual statements. The tasteful furnishings place the family's status well above the average. Paintings and prints abound. Although less opulent than the expansive interiors of the wealthy homes in *Dallas* and *Dynasty*, the environment and lifestyle of the Huxtables clearly witness to the aspirations and concepts of the good life that most Americans associate with success. The master bedroom is spacious, and the children have their own rooms. Seeing family members moving down hallways into various places can communicate certain aspects of family life. Watching Theo, for instance, leave his room and bound down the ample stairway to join his family suggests the comfort of both privacy and sharing. The large living room easily accommodates the family, grandparents, and guests.

Many scenes, however, take place in the kitchen. Its fluid, open space allows for a constant stream of people and various gatherings, as well as for family dining. Behind the large table is an open fireplace.

Myths of the American Way permeate *The Cosby Show* with tales we like to see and hear. Blacks become outstanding professionals, community leaders, living in integrated neighborhoods where their children play freely with children of other races. The positive, family-centered episodes that appear each week are frequently conceived and supervised by Bill Cosby, who is also the principal actor. In his genius for comedy, his extraordinary way with children, and his personal interest in images of parenthood, Cosby reminds one of Norman Rockwell early in the century. The significant difference is that the heroes and heroines of these tales of the good life are members of a black family and Cosby himself is part of the symbolic portraiture. Whether or not the images are truly representative of black or white contemporary families, the narratives are comforting and reassuring. Amid the disorders of ordinary living—the increase of families below the poverty level and the steady rise in homelessness in American society—"entertainment" in this instance becomes a mythic fable of what might be.

There are other types of shows which fly in the face of "reality," and yet provide mythic and moral narratives. Some of them focus on the kinds of changes that are supposedly occurring in American society. Gloria Steinem wrote a brief article for *TV Guide* describing *Cagney and Lacey* as the best show on television,[5] and those who have followed the series since it began in 1982 have recognized a different kind of symbolic representation. Here are two women whose lives are shown largely

---

5 Gloria Steinem, "Why I Consider *Cagney & Lacey* the Best Show on TV," *TV Guide* (January 16, 1988), pp. 4-6.

The Electronic Golden Calf

outside the home as they carry out their professional commitments. Early fans saw these women as new heroines in their role as policewomen, giving a different twist to the genre of police dramas. The domestic status of each—one happily married, the other single—was a secondary, minor motif. Steinem notes that the series represents a departure from the trivial assumptions that women cannot get along with one another and that they are essentially a part of a man's world, rivaling each other for his affections.

The show has been applauded not only for the role models it presents, but also for the daring presentation of themes that bring controversial topics into public discourse. Departing from screeching tires and shootouts, *Cagney and Lacey* may be compared to another highly respected show from earlier seasons, *Hill Street Blues*. Both have dealt with highly sensitive issues that seldom appear on television: alcoholism, abortion, and date rape. Many critics have applauded the moving protrayal by Sharon Gless as Cagney, facing a potential problem with alcohol. After her alcoholic father dies following a fall in his apartment, a wake is held in Flannery's Bar. The bereft daughter repeatedly toasts his memory with drinks. Recalling other episodes in which Lacey has gently chided Cagney about her drinking, viewers have an uneasy feeling that alcoholism is a potential threat for her.

The show also received praises for giving alternative images of marriage and family. Lacey's husband, Harvey, is a blue-collar worker married to an independent woman following a nontraditional profession. Viewers also see a policewoman as mother: Lacey takes a maternity leave from the force to have her third child. In one program Lacey, about to deliver at any moment, resumes her role as policewoman in tracking down a hit-and-run driver. Harvey, concerned about her condition, joins Cagney in the detective work while Lacey orchestrates the search from their Queens apartment. Later we see the tensions that arise over the care of children when both parents work, as Harvey and Lacey deal with parenting and family responsibilities. Although the themes explored in *Cagney and Lacey* have a harsher ring than those of *The Cosby Show*, they too are mythic in that they provide tangible symbols for changing expectations of women and thinking about women. Even when conflicts are not resolved, as in the issue of abortion, alternative views, through their symbolization in this powerful medium, become more comprehensible.

Since mythic authority asserts itself through repeated stories, the soap operas play a unique role in our culture. Here are daily, continuous patterns of tales which entertain while they dramatize social dynamics and role models. For an hour or more, soap operas move slowly, almost dully (like real life), through conflicts and tensions. While usually comfortably middle-class, these heroes and heroines, frequently employed as doctors and lawyers, engage endlessly in conversations and crises: intrigue, infidelity, surgery, nervous breakdowns, having children or deciding not to have them, running away, making up, terminal illness, getting married, getting divorced, separation, death, abortion, alcoholism, and amnesia. Human relationships and the value decisions which radiate from them are the stuff of soap operas. Their slow pace and the relatively constant cast of performers enable viewers to keep up with the stories, even if one or two episodes are missed. For avid fans *Soap Opera Digest* is published weekly, with reviews of previous programs and articles that speculate on future events and decisions which leading characters may make. Like fanciful tales and gossip that surround political, religious, or cultural dignitaries, these webs of fantasy confer an almost lifelike quality on fictional heroes and heroines of the daytime dramas. Through their prolonged daily exposure, fictional characters become surrogate household members and provide common bonds among those who watch the same soap opera.

The Electronic Golden Calf

The morality plays of "soaps" dramatize the interaction between good and evil in easily understood terms. Unlike traditional myths, however, they do not resolve conflicts in a single episode. Rather, they are open-ended, more like life itself. The viewer moves with the characters through their lives and changing circumstances. In long-running shows, such as *All My Children*, changing social attitudes are reflected in the characters and their human problems. In recent years daytime dramas have portrayed increased sexual freedom, and several have dealt with the topic of homosexuality. As the AIDS phenomenon erupted in real life, some soaps introduced this into their make-believe tragedies. Working their way slowly through time, these lifelike melodramas—ordinary and extraordinary—provide a constant audio-visual hum of moral tales every weekday afternoon. After weeks, sometimes months, in the end the good prevails, pausing only momentarily in triumph before the shadows of evil appear again. These leisurely everyday dramas take us through a moral meandering over an indefinite span of time and, as in life, the resolutions are tentative and fragile.

In contrast to soap operas, another type of mythic tale, the commercial, telescopes and compresses decision and action into a few brief seconds. Terse, fast-action sequences about things we need or desire constitute its basic structure. Although viewers may disdain them, they provide the networks with their basic revenue. They have become an integral part of most broadcasting in the United States, permeating all kinds of programs. Mini-dramas about the good life, the commercials draw from a wide range of themes: good fellowship and friendship, warm family ties and loving relationships between parents and children, success in professional life, pride in personal looks and the anticipation of constant improvement, the accumulation of possessions for comfort and for the minimization of work, the achievement of social status, the enhancement of personal growth and performance, patriotism and pride in community, the privilege of choice and the positive values of competition. These motifs are frequently combined with national celebrations, sports events, or conventional holidays.

Several years ago American Telephone and Telegraph commercials linked a wide range of human emotions to a telephone call. "Reach out and touch someone" became a familiar phrase associated with bringing together family members who might be separated by distance, great or small. In a matter of seconds an electronic family portrait was sketched. Over time one might see many different age and ethnic groupings, but the families portrayed depended upon the telephone to maintain close ties. The occasions for calling might be to celebrate, to surprise, or to nurture. Extending this tradition in a special way, New England Telephone sponsored a sequence of ads through which a dramatic narrative of family reconciliation evolved. During a period of about three months a series of thirty-second commercials was released, each building upon the previous to add more details to the unfolding story.

Each commercial of the series began with a title and episode similar to the opening captions of a drama or mini-series. "The Family, Part I" showed a young professional woman calling home. After speaking about her new apartment, Kathy tells her parents that she has talked to her sister Jill. The father then abruptly hangs up. Mom says, "I'm here. You know he doesn't like to talk about your sister." Kathy concludes the conversation by saying, "Mom, we all have to start talking." The commercial ends with the familiar logo of New England Telephone superimposed over a spatial view of New England and their familiar tune: "We're the one for you, New England, New England Telephone."

After this first act of the drama had been repeatedly shown on prime-time, "The Family, Part II," appeared. The second of the series featured a conversation between Kathy and her dad. He has called to apologize for hanging up. In their conversation we find out a little more about the conflict. Dad says, "I still can't believe she left like that." Kathy responds, "Well, you didn't give her much choice. But," she adds, "you really miss her, don't you?" Once more the logo and singer: "We're the one for you, New England...."

In "The Family, Part III" we see and hear the two sisters, Kathy and Jill, speaking on the phone to each other. Kathy opens the conversation: "Jill, you gotta call Dad. I know he was wrong about you and Jeff." Jill protests, saying he should call her. Kathy admits she's right, "But you know Dad. He can't call. He misses you." She pleads with her sister, but Jill says, "I can't." The third episode thus ends on a note of despair as Kathy sadly acknowledges, "It's been two years. If one of you isn't big enough to make that call, it's going be a lifetime." Logo and music have now become a kind of "curtain" that brings each act of the drama to an end. "We're the one for you...."

By this time interested viewers had followed these scenes of family conflict through the entire fall. Finally it all ended happily when the final episode was aired on Christmas Day, 1988. This dramatization ran sixty seconds, twice the length of the earlier ones. There we see all four members of the family. Mom hears the phone ringing and asks Dad to get it. The two sisters are together, but Jill has initiated the call. "How are you?" Dad: "I'm good." Jill speaks, "I'm good, too....I...uh...wanted to call many times. It's been two years now." Dad then tells his estranged daughter that he was wrong, and that he had no right to interfere in her life. "I'm sorry," he says, and Jill responds, "I've missed you so much, Dad." The final image shows a radiant Kathy as she witnesses the reconciliation. The music added the final, familiar blessing, "We're the one...." Good commercials, like successful moral tales, make us feel good. In stories and in jingles they invite us to join in the fun or share the idealism.

The series of New England Telephone commercials is self-contained, without specific reference to time and place. In addition, it presents abstract social types who fit into certain demo-graphic categories with predictable consumer patterns. The story and images allowed us to recognize something familiar: a family in conflict. At the start, father and daughter no longer speak to each other. Suspense is built through a series of conver-sations, and at the end is the hoped-for reconciliation. The human drama directly featured has received our primary atten-tion. Indirectly promoted, yet a key factor in the exchanges and final resolutions, is the telephone, frequently used by family members.

Media analyst Michael Schudson has contrasted this more abstract idealized advertising with direct, particularized local ads. When a department store announces a sale, the main task of the ad is to identify the products plainly and simply and to call attention to the bargains. National advertising, in contrast, is more indirect.

> The commercial for Coca-Cola or Alka Seltzer does not say how the consumer can buy the advertised product; it does not typically announce a phone number to call or a place to shop....It is a general re-minder or reinforcer, not an urgent appeal to go out and buy.[6]

In order for an indirect advertisement to be successful viewers must be drawn directly into the primary drama. This depends upon the creation of "typical" situations—ones which viewers can easily identify. Thus the creators of commercials must suppress the eccentric qualities that actually distinguish families and individuals. Their job is to build bridges of recognition to millions of viewers. These modern image-makers, like their aca-demic counterparts in earlier centuries, have to fashion highly

---

6 Michael Schudson, *Advertising, the Uneasy Persuasion: Its Dubious Impact on Ameri-can Society* (New York: Basic Books, 1984), p. 211.

The Electronic Golden Calf

conventional symbols which provide the illusion of authenticity and familiarity. In these commercials we see symbolic representations of a middle to upper-middle-class family. Their portraits—speech, dress, action—and their environments have to be carefully abstracted so that viewers might recognize them as "reality." At the same time these generalized portrayals must be sufficiently particular to avoid empty stereotyping.

Schudson links these aesthetic conventions of advertising to the political economy and the values it celebrates and promotes, calling this "capitalist realism." This he compares to socialist realism and the ways in which Soviet artists and writers use a particular aesthetic style to communicate significant themes. Permeating the stylistic devices is the fundamental orientation to buying and selling. Schudson, for instance, contends that advertising is an important way in which this society materializes its experiences. People, he says, need "to see in pictures or hear in words even what they already know as deeply as they know anything, *especially* what they know as deeply as they know anything....This is equally true of large social systems. Advertising is capitalism's way of saying 'I love you' to itself."[7]

From modestly designed ads in small newspapers to high-tech video commercials, advertising reaffirms the values we associate with the good life and reassures us that these are constant and obtainable. Advertising, like the older church or state-sponsored art, celebrates and euologizes the system that subsidizes it.

Commercials, sitcoms, and soaps imaginatively visualize what we find worthy or unworthy, yet we regard these as "make believe." Other TV images are described as "real." For instance, many viewers accept the news programs as a way of finding out

---

[7] *Ibid.*, pp. 231-232.

what's happening in the world. But these, too, are symbolic and selective and reveal what our society values and disvalues.

Shaping Reality

"What is going on?" is an essentially human question. Throughout time it has been asked wherever life is shared—in the family, neighborhood, city, and nation. Today television enables the question to be raised throughout the universe. TV sets may bring into individual homes audio-visual reports of what is going on around the world, as well as in space. As McLuhan and others anticipated, the information revolutions— print and electronic—have transformed both our sense of community and our perspective on "reality." Within hours, sometimes minutes, we have sights and sounds of events in distant places which may evoke fear, anguish, sympathy, and responsive action.

In premodern times religious and political leaders were careful to select the events that were publicly proclaimed, events that affected the lives of everyone. These were memorialized on buildings and monuments in carved and painted images. In the classical world, for example, important military victories were narrated on columns and triumphant arches as well as on temples. In the Middle Ages, cathedrals were decorated with images that described the significant happenings that governed and ordered life. One of the ambulatory stained glass windows at Chartres depicts events in the life of the emperor Charlemagne; its various sections illustrate his importance to the development of the church. On the exterior, three portals give an overview of history. Sculpted figures represent the heroes of the Old Testament and historical circumstances which culminate in the reign of Christ. Leading up to the doorways on the southern entrance are images of the saints, martyrs, and servants of the church since the time of Christ. Selected by an ecclesiastical hierarchy and executed by artisans, the stone and glass symbols of

121

The Electronic Golden Calf

Chartres, like the sculptures on the facade of the Parthenon, were visual constructions of meaning. The exigencies of daily life—political, social, and economic—might be far removed from this idealized order of images. Moreover, persons who could write about such visual symbols were, like Suger and Bernard, a literate, clerical elite. We do not know how the illiterate responded or whether persons found these symbols a contradiction or confirmation of their experiences.

In addition to these "reports" in stone and glass, the medieval Christian learned about the shape of reality through ritual and sermon. In the course of the liturgy, knowledge about human life and destiny was communicated through the unfolding of the ritual of the eucharist. Readings from the Bible described in words many of the same incidents that could be seen in the colored images and statuary. Through the sermon the day-to-day events of the local community, as well as wars or plagues, would be placed in the larger context of the Christian drama of salvation. That cosmic narrative provided the continous framework which encompassed the past and present and anticipated future events.

Thus the contours of reality were formed to include the time and space of two spheres—the natural and supernatural. Long before literacy and the mass media, mythological "pictures of reality" were presented in dramatic narrative, enhanced by visual and musical forms. A symbolic world gave significance to personal experiences, the community, and the universe. Rituals and myths identified friends, foes, and a communal destiny. Today no overarching canopy of religious belief circumscribes and explains the whole of daily life.

Throughout United States history public access to information and the right to free speech and press has enabled news institutions to assume the responsibility for giving open answers to the question: "What is going on?" Moreover, the role of newspapers has become increasingly important as the population of the country grows more religiously, racially, and ethnically complex. As early as the nineteenth century Alexis de Toqueville recognized the ways in which newspapers became a unifying, symbolizing agent. In contrast to their role in aristocracies, newspapers are particularly vital to democracies. They become the source of shared knowledge and can identify common interests and needs for action. Without knowing each other, strangers may talk every day and make decisions without ever meeting. "The newspaper," wrote this French observer of American society, "comes of its own accord and talks to you briefly every day on the common weal, without distracting you from your private affairs." He compares the newspaper to a beacon which unites wandering minds. "Only a newspaper," he said, can "drop the same thought into a thousand minds at the same moment."[8]

Written over a hundred and fifty years ago, these remarks are equally useful today in pointing out the authoritative role of news agencies in fabricating our collective symbols of reality. Reading on a crowded subway or bus, picking up the paper from the mail box in an isolated rural area, or turning on the TV newscasts are actions that link Americans with one another. In this respect, television is especially powerful. As persons watch the news, they are aware that others are also watching and that there will be common subjects and events to discuss. Shared perceptions draw separate individuals into a fragile and illusory order which otherwise would not exist. Amid fragmented constituencies—religious, political, and economic—the mass media attempt to portray significant events and provide information, helping us to understand ourselves and our complex society.

---

8 Alexis de Tocqueville, "On the Relation Between Public Associations and the Newspapers," *Democracy in America"*, *vol 2* (New York: Vintage Books, 1958), pp. 119-122.

The Electronic Golden Calf

The nightly news programs, for example, present accounts of "reality," carefully constructed narratives made up of both words and images that explain what is happening in the world. The success of television's ritualistic orientation may be measured by the fact that most of us do not view the "news" as a symbolic construction, but as an essentially believable reality.[9]

Each of the three major networks in the United States condenses national and international news into a thirty-minute program interlaced with advertisements. The rhythm, pattern, and composition of news stories into a dramatic whole heighten their ritualistic qualities.

Every day for a limited, carefully orchestrated period of time our attention is drawn to highly concentrated *symbolic reports* of events. These thirty-minute distillations, unlike detailed, lengthy explanations, give us a sense of the totality of things—a selective, fabricated view of "reality." What we actually view are shared symbols of the real world. We may know very little about what is happening in, say, Nicaragua, the Middle East, or Washington, D.C., but we grasp certain symbolic representations which become the basis of thinking, acting, and voting. Without prolonged reading or investigation, constant viewers of television are indoctrinated through words and pictures into a world view. When TV's words and pictures are our only source of information about the lives of people in distant countries, their land, government, and living conditions, the stakes are high. In a free society, a great responsibility rests on those who produce news programs.

---

[9] See *The People and the Press: A Times Mirror Investigation of Public Attitudes Toward the News Media*, conducted by the Gallup Organization (Los Angeles: Times Mirror, 1986). The survey showed that the network anchors are considered believable by about ninety percent of the American population.

Americans depend on a special kind of authority figure, the "anchor-person"—the man or woman who leads viewers through intensive, patterned reporting of events. Heralded by ceremonial sounds and silhouetted against global symbols, the anchors introduce the program and sustain the connecting link running through the montage of news stories. Their familiar faces and voices predominate during a half hour in which audiences get an overview of worldwide happenings. In their commanding roles they appear to sort out the momentous from the less momentous occurrences that go on in the universe. Networks are aware that these persons must be perceived as trustworthy. The credibility of the stories and the seriousness with which we respond to them are closely linked to our belief that the information is "true."

It has been argued, however, that the system is not as open as it should be. That is, what we see—or more important, what we don't see—distorts reality. The precise effects of press coverage are not easily determined, but we can examine more closely its power to select the issues that are publicly represented and discussed. Several critics have claimed that the mass media, especially television, promote an illusory perception of reality and tend to generate uniformity of opinion. The selective presentation of information limits, even manipulates, public debate.

To consider these issues we need to look at television as a symbolizing process: first, the selection involved in camerawork and editing, and second, the composition of diverse portions of news footage into a carefully fabricated whole.

The Symbolizing Process

The creation of images in all media—painting, photography, sculpture, graphic arts—is essentially a selective process. None of the visual arts, including television, can present reality. Instead they all re-present experience, selecting certain things to emphasize while ignoring many others. Yet photography, film,

The Electronic Golden Calf

and particularly television appear to have a special claim on authenticity. In a portrait or landscape painting we may, of course, recognize the subject; but however "life-like" the image, the hand of the creator is evident. Whether we are looking at a contemporary neo-realist or a fifteenth-century Flemish work, we can observe how the artist works to give the impression of a human face or figure. Separating the reality of the person from the image itself are the painter's brushstrokes and pigments, and we accept the fact that the artist has revealed certain things and concealed others. Most viewers presume the presence of the artist as mediator, negotiating reality for us through the form.

Photography, film, and television, by contrast, appear to unveil material existence and join viewers in a one-to-one relationship to it. The presence of the mediator is not so readily detected. These media seem to be more "objective." We assume that the camera lens, like that of our own eye, is a transparent agent through which the world yields its palpable truths. This analogy between human and mechanical lens helps to support the false notion that these media are innocent observers that capture reality as it unfolds. Since film and television involve moving images, we find even stronger associations between these images and our own experience. Yet to comprehend the authoritative power of news programs we need to be conscious of the creative, selective process involved in the *re*-presentation of events that flow across the TV screen. Images that *seem* to put us directly in touch with distant places and events only appear because control—both technical and editorial—has been exerted at several levels.

Before the hand-held camera was improved, we still could sense the human being behind it. Today, however, sophisticated visual equipment may pick up the most intimate detail with steady precision; the hand is invisible. More surrealistic than realistic, the camera can switch in mini-seconds from the most intimate portraiture—partial views which isolate and frame portions of the human face—to distant views of masses of people. By manipulating the lens, camera people can create images of a whole that is in fact as circumscribed as the stretched canvas of a landscape painting. Far from conveying reality, the process is synthetic; like other media, TV relies on highly selective procedures in the composition of its images.

Film analyst Jeremy Murray-Brown has described "the cut" as the most fundamental technical device used in television, one that determines "the hidden message of the medium, as type does with print, and rhyme and meter do in poetry." From the shift of the camera from one angle to another comes a message to the viewer to look for meaning. Murray-Brown points out that through the cut one image is linked to another to form a webbing of pictures that has been artificially created. Here is the hand of the artist at work, selecting and mixing in ways comparable to the painter's organization of lines, colors, and textures. Moreover, the sound—often the voice of the commentator—gives the excuse for the cut. These interactions between sight and sound become a "complex relationship of the two senses like the intertwining of the DNA helix."[10] Since news stories are relatively short and must be dramatic, the cut becomes the organizing principle governing their pace and emphasis. Each news segment is thus an independent montage which, along with the commercials, must be fitted by its editor into a thirty-minute program.

The integration of selected parts into a whole is another important dimension of the symbolizing process. All artists understand what it is to compose, to frame subjects, organizing them into a coherent pattern, and television news is no exception. However, this organizing process is especially sensitive since

---

[10] Jeremy Murray-Brown, "Video Ergo Sum," in *Video Icons and Values* (forthcoming 1990).

The Electronic Golden Calf

viewers are looking for "reality"—"What is going on?"—not *symbols* of reality. Yet how the world looks and sounds on TV news programs depends upon which events have been artfully distilled, selected, and framed into this tightly packaged composition. As more and more Americans look to TV news for information, a common question critics raise is, "Which people, places, and happenings are chosen to represent the reality of the day?" How does TV news distort the shape of reality?

To give one example, in the fall of 1988 respected TV anchorman Ted Koppel raised the question of why American TV covers the Third World as it does. Discussing this issue with him were Ambassador Oumarou Youssouffou, from the Organization of African Unity, Lawrence Grossman, former president of NBC News, and Alexander Cockburn, writer for *The Wall Street Journal* and *The Nation*. Ambassador Youssouffou offered several illustrations of the problem. He noted that the hatching of a rare condor egg in California received as much as or more reporting than a continent of four hundred million people. Even the tragic events and loss of life in Burundi, Mozambique and Ethiopia seemed of little interest to the viewing public. Youssoufrou was especially concerned about racist overtones and pointed to the prominent attention given to violence against whites, as contrasted to the under-reporting of assaults upon non-whites. While what happens to a white farmer in Mozambique or South Africa becomes front page news, he observed, it takes a massive massacre of blacks to merit comparable reporting.

Both Grossman and Cockburn agreed with Koppel's assessment that there is even less coverage of the Third World today than there was ten years ago. Lawrence Grossman commented that there are NBC news bureaus and correspondents in all the major capitols of Western Europe, yet only one NBC correspondent in all of Africa—in South Africa—and none in South America. He noted also that even editors and professional journalists have little historical or any other knowledge about many of these remote, yet important, places. The general public, moreover, appears both uninformed and uninterested. Alexander Cockburn added that TV news programs—and to an extent, the press in general—have become a form of entertainment rather than a source of information.

Cockburn brought up the role of government in determining news coverage. The agenda of the President or the State Department enables certain parts of the world to leap into prominence and then vanish from the headlines, and frequently from public concern. Our shifting political and diplomatic ventures—in Indonesia, Central and South America, and Afghanistan—draw attention to particular places and events. One country may be featured prominently for weeks, even months, only to disappear from the news completely. Cockburn suggested that with the easing of tensions between the Soviet Union and the United States, the reporting of Third World people and events might move in new directions, such as world ecology and the problems of Third World economies.

In his remarks Cockburn made the point that TV news is presented in symbolic terms, a concept which a number of other critics have pursued. In her book, *Making News*, Gaye Tuchman, for example, describes news as a "web of facticity." She contends that rather than representing society and its social structures, newspersons and institutions actively create symbolic world views. These serve as a "window on the world" through which news consumers perceive reality. She asks: Who creates these windows and where are they placed? Does a window have many panes or few? Are they clear or opaque? Since worlds of private and communal experience are, in fact, almost limitless in number, which ones are selected to be disclosed? The essence of the news-windows, Tuchman concludes, is their capacity to

The Electronic Golden Calf

symbolize and to set limits to what is perceived as the "real" world.[11]

For some critics our information system is flawed not simply by the symbolic packaging of news, but also by the way that some stories are played down or suppressed. They argue that our world views may be significantly distorted by what we don't know. Countries undergoing painful conflicts have attempted to stifle outside condemnation by eliminating the modern icono-clast—an open press. South Africa has succeeded in suppressing the powerful images that kept its apartheid policy in the minds and consciousness of millions of viewers in the west. In most na-tions, however, images of authority are controlled in more in-direct ways, which can take many forms.

In the 1980s the debate about the effect of the media cover-age of the Vietnam war was still going on, and governments were cautious about press coverage of military conflicts. Taking no chances on how the press might report the invasion of Granada, the Reagan adminstration barred reporters from the scene. Correspondents who defied the ban and tried to get there were turned back by the military; television coverage was sup-plied by the Armed Forces. Four years later, in 1988, a Front Line documentary, "Granada," written by journalist Seymour Hirsch and produced by PBS, critically scrutinized the invasion itself. Among other things it reported that the invasion, coming soon after the tragic bombing of the American barracks in Le-banon, seemed crucial for restoring the authoritative image of President Reagan just prior to the election of 1984.

The public became aware of a special kind of image manage-ment called "disinformation" in 1986. In October of that year, the press disclosed a memo from White House national security

---

[11] Gaye Tuchman, *Making News: A Study in the Construction of Reality* (New York: The Free Press, 1978), pp. 182-197

advisor John M. Poindexter to Ronald Reagan on a strategy that would assist the administration in its Libyan policy. In his memo to the President, Poindexter explained how it could be used against Libyan leader Moammar Khadafy. The essential factor in disinformation strategy is the combination of real and illusory events to influence the public's perception of reality. Poindexter argued that the government had a right to use disinformation as a strategy to protect national security. Denying that it was intended to deceive the press or public in the United States or elsewhere, he still conceded that some people might have been deceived.

Upon disclosure of the Poindexter disinformation campaign, both conservative and liberal commentators objected to the government's abuse of the American press. Most argued that the freedom of the press in the United States depends upon the credibility of information from the government. Discussion of Poindexter's tactics was cut short by even more shocking revelations of the Iran-contra scandal, which was again traced to the President's national security advisors. These latter disclosures would momentarily deface the trustworthy, "take-charge" portraits of Ronald Reagan.

To counter the image-making power of news institutions, media experts in the White House now specialize in political portraiture. At times situations arise which dramatically illustrate certain struggles between these two major symbol-makers. As part of Ronald Reagan's itinerary at an economic summit in 1985, he and West German Chancellor Helmut Kohl were to place a double wreath at a military cemetery. The event was billed as a symbol of reconciliation and a celebration of forty years of peace. In advance planning for the trip, however, Reagan aides had failed to notice that among those buried at Bitburg Cemetery were members of the elite Nazi SS Corps. Once this became known, there were outbursts of anger and resentment. Stories appeared daily in the national and world

The Electronic Golden Calf

press. The gesture that was meant to symbolize peace and friendship began instead to awaken painful memories of Nazi atrocities, especially the Holocaust. Internationally known Jewish leaders such as Elie Wiesel directly appealed to the President to cancel the graveside ceremony. The House of Representatives took up a resolution to call off the cemetery visit; the ensuing debate further inflamed the situation. National pollsters jumped in, and their studies showed widespread criticism of the Bitburg trip.

Despite the protests, the President held fast to his decision; he blamed the media for stirring up the controversy. It was, he said, "morally right" for him to go; he continued to emphasize the visit as a symbol of reconciliation. Michael Deaver went over a day ahead of time to make sure that pictures of the ceremony itself would not do further damage. Martin Linsky noted that the conflicts which sometimes arise between politicians and reporters may be summed up by the placement of the "tripod" at Bitburg. The spot chosen by network people would have allowed cameras to frame Reagan against the background of the SS graves, while administration people were adamant that the tripod be positioned so that no inclusive visual perspectives were possible.

The ceremony took place, and the Nazi graves did not show in the formal clips of the event. Its length of time was reduced from twenty to eight minutes. Reagan and Kohl walked separately, each accompanied by a military officer. The leaders placed their wreaths and the generals shook hands over the grave. Reagan's motorcade then took off, leaving out of sight the groups of Germans protesting this event. But on the nightly news programs American viewers saw not only excerpts of the ceremony, but protests in the streets of Germany, Miami, Washington, D.C., California, and Israel as well.

Yet the final victor in this tug of symbols appears to have been the President. Bitburg was but one ceremonial stop, for also televised on the evening news were the other symbolic visits he made that day. Traveling to a US airbase where he eulogized the American soldiers who fell in World War II, Reagan brought up the Holocaust and its terror. Reconciliation does not mean forgetting, he said. "I promise you we will never forget." Later he visited the grave of Conrad Adenaur, the first post-war Chancellor, a man known for his opposition to Hitler. Then he and Mrs. Reagan made an unscheduled visit to Bergen-Belsen, the concentration camp where fifty thousand Jews had been exterminated. Among these somber ruins he spoke again of Holocaust victims: "Here they lie, never to hope, never to love, never to pray, never to heal, never to laugh, never to cry...." And in closing he quoted from *The Diary of a Young Girl* by Anne Frank, who had died there.

This use of visual symbols to enhance the position of rulers and politicians is not new. Throughout history heads of empires and states have employed artists to create symbols of authority which depict the order they represent and uphold. The communications revolution has brought images in different forms, but their function has remained the same: to render visible and thus objectify the invisible values that characterize a community and its leadership. Television is indispensible today to those who seek and would maintain political power.

Symbols of Political Authority

Emperors and politicians of the classical world, rulers of the early medieval church-state, and European monarchs have been portrayed in various ways as symbols of authority. Athens and Rome were filled with statues of famous leaders, and rulers of the Holy Roman Empire developed similar images. One example from the sixth century is particularly impressive, a mosaic depicting the Emperor Justinian, head of both church and empire, in the sanctuary of San Vitale, Ravenna. There, with ecclesiastical leaders to his left and civil servants and soldiers to

The Electronic Golden Calf

his right, Justinian stands as the supreme earthly ruler and highest priestly power. On the opposite wall is the Empress Theodora and her retinue. Together they rule Christendom. Above the royal symbols are mosaics which present the heroic leaders of the Bible—Moses, Abraham, Jacob, and the four evangelists, Matthew, Mark, Luke, and John. Overarching these multi-level groupings of sacred figures hovers a vaulted canopy, lavish patterns of colors and shapes. Just beyond the pictorial procession formed by Justinian and Theodora stands the altar: above it is another shimmering mosaic in the apse. It shows a figure of Christ enthroned, seated between two archangels. He presents a martyr's crown to San Vitale; on his left, Bishop Ec-clesius offers him a model of the church.

How sixth-century worshippers might perceive and respond to this incredibly rich panoply of symbols cannot be precisely known. Was this imperial couple supposed to participate in the ritual, offering the bread and wine of the eucharist? Or were they being depicted as benefactors of the church presenting generous gifts? Though interpretations may vary, these mosaics are a vivid example of the visual representation of political power, one which appears to have reached into the sacred and secular realms.[12]

As we examine contemporary symbols of authority we shall ask: How do politicians in a technological, democratic, and secular society use images to enhance their position? The media for modern political portraiture are not paint, stone, and mosaics but photography, film, and especially television. As politicians began to grasp the potential of television to reach millions of viewers and voters, the production of modern images

---

[12] Kitzinger, *Byzantine Art*, pp. 87-88. Kitzinger observes that Justinian's figure seems to dominate. Yet Archbishop Maximianus is depicted as a taller figure and appears to be standing in front of the emperor.

of power rose dramatically. Our contemporary leaders are now portrayed on a scale comparable to the rulers of the ancient world. Replacing the sculptors, stone cutters, and painters of today are publicity firms, media managers, and TV journalists.

Like ancient priest-kings and medieval clerics, modern American politicians also participate in rituals and employ myths. But they do not claim to draw us into the supernatural order. Nor do they return us to the dawn of creation and the birth of the gods, or enable us to participate in resurrection. Instead, through the mass media they address the human need for an ordered universe and present themselves as trusted leaders who represent and defend a people's highest aspirations. In ceremonial speeches politicians remind us of the origins and visions of American society and echo the early settlers' religious convictions and views of America as the New Eden. Liberty and equality, the primary themes of this gospel, are frequently used to explain domestic and foreign policies.

During the twentieth century communication technologies have enabled politicians to establish instantaneously a sense of their presence. In the 1930s Franklin D. Roosevelt used radio to transcend barriers of time and space, becoming a "live" voice in family homes throughout the nation. John F. Kennedy was the first American president to benefit from television's capacity to draw viewers into the innermost spaces of political rites in which they immediately "participated" by seeing and hearing. In contrast, the loyal supporters of earlier rulers had only static images that *re-told* ceremonial events. Today the television medium both presents and re-presents events even as they happen, creating a unique kind of authoritative image. No other American president, including Kennedy, has been as skilled as Ronald Reagan and his advisors in crafting images of leadership suitable for the new technology.

The Electronic Golden Calf

Iconified Politics

Seated behind his desk in the Oval Office Ronald Reagan presented his farewell to the nation.[13] He spoke of the revolution he had initiated. One of its greatest accomplishments, Reagan told us, was the rediscovery of American values and the restoration of national pride and patriotism. He warned that a loss of the "American memory" would result in an erosion of the country's spirit. "If we forget what we did, we won't know who we are." Our spirit is back, he asserted, but it must be reinstitutionalized. To accomplish this we need to pay more attention to American history, focusing not on fashion but on what is important. We should, he proposed, have "greater emphasis of civic ritual." Finally, Reagan observed that all great changes begin at the family dinner table, where parents talk to their children about what it means to be an American. Earlier in our national life patriotism was expressed in the family, in the neighborhood and in popular culture. That must happen again, insisted the President. In closing, the chief executive credited the success of his value revolution to "you, the people." "Reagan's regiments" are the decent, ordinary citizens who supported him and restored faith and confidence in the nation's ideals.

The accomplishments of "Reagan's regiments," however, would not have been possible without the medium of television and the movie actor/politician's masterful understanding and practice of "civic ritual." Whether or not Reagan and his aides deliberately set it up, they succeeded in finding ways to ritualize events and to construct pervasive, moving images of authority. In a religiously plural, or for some, a "secular" society, many of

---

[13] Ronald Reagan's farewell address to the nation was telecast January 12, 1989. The text released by the White House also appeared in the *New York Times* on the same day.

the "photo opportunities" became occasions for civic rituals.[14] Television has enormous power to create modern icons of political authority. To grasp the power of secular rituals we have to shift our view from high art—mosaics of Justinian and Theodora—to the nightly news clips and special network reports in which we can discover contemporary symbols of power.

Throughout the eight years of the Reagan era ceremonial images were carefully fabricated to communicate and promote the philosophy, values, and authority of the President. The following examples will illustrate how television symbols were designed to reinforce the principles and influence of the president. They were fleeting and impressionistic, but they were also steady and pervasive, and for eight years they saturated our society. Cumulatively, these images formed a giant media mosaic more impressive than the colossal statues of the ancient emperors. From the beginning of his first term Ronald Reagan used the television medium to leap over congressional opposition and barriers and present his image and ideology to "you, the people."

One of Reagan's first major victories was a change in the nation's tax laws, early in 1981. Ostensibly he reduced the taxes of all citizens, but he was most effective in relieving the tax burden of the wealthy. The signing of this bill was presented to viewers of the evening news program, but it might easily have been mistaken for a scene from the popular drama *Dallas*. The locale was

---

[14] Anthropologists can help us to understand the power of modern secular ceremonies by pointing out their affinities to earlier rites. Ritual action performed an integrative function in primitive societies, but in a complex, secular world, it has become fragmented. The power and dynamics of traditional ritual have migrated, Victor Turner observes, "directly or in disguise" into other domains such as politics, aesthetics, law, and popular culture. See Victor Turner, "Variation on the Theme of Liminality," in *Secular Rituals*, Sally F. Moore and Barbara G. Myerhoff, eds. (Amsterdam: Van Gorcum & Co., 1977).

The Electronic Golden Calf

the President's ranch in California, alive with reporters and electronic equipment. A lean, cowboy President in jeans and boots strode out of his ranch house and over to an outdoor desk piled with papers to sign. There, pen in hand, he "conquered" the real enemy: taxes. Meanwhile on the sidelines, the first lady, also in ranch attire, struggled with the family dog as journalists scrambled for a better view of the President. Here was the best of the American myth: leader sets people free from taxes as first lady looks on admiringly.

(Yet even as the event was telecast, it was becoming clear to at least one advisor that this tax strategy might not work. David Stockman, original advocate of the fiscal policy, subsequently leaked the bad news and five years later wrote a book about the problems of the Reagan revolution. Stockman described how fictitious economic growth rates had been used to justify the tax cuts and to cover up the massive deficit inherent in the so-called supply-side economic policy.)

Television has made it possible for millions of people to participate to some degree in significant political ceremonies like this one. The dynamics of some of these televised events recall traditional forms of religious communication. For example, the traditional model, in which a sacred event is reenacted within carefully measured boundaries of time and space, is paralleled in the formal structures of sports events and civil ceremonies such as the Super Bowl football game and inauguration of the President.

When, through an unusual coincidence in 1985, President Reagan's second inauguration was telecast on the same day as the Super Bowl game, the entire day seemed liturgically orchestrated. Viewers were taken from one sacred event to another. As the President was sworn into his second term, millions of viewers shared, through TV, in a solemn event in the life of the nation. Later that day, by the miracle of technology, two sacred spaces—the White House and the Super Bowl stadium—were united. In the White House President Reagan tossed a coin to start the game across the continent. The newly inaugurated commander-in-chief ceremoniously opened the event that symbolizes to many the value of competition and the importance of being "Number One." Standing before a large landscape painting of the American West, Ronald Reagan seemed to personify the heroic image of a winner. Later, thousands of miles away, between halves of the game, entertainment reinforced patriotic sentiments as marching bands and drill teams formed a huge American flag on the football field. The TV screen offered yet one more exchange, when the President, again standing in front of the rugged landscape painting, spoke on the telephone to the victorious football coach.

In various ways the charismatic Reagan broke the bonds of time, space, and institutional structures; through the medium of television, he addressed the believers—the American public—directly. Magazines and newspapers combined with television to form a monumental collection of authoritative images that fashioned the bigger-than-life portrait of a leader. Through carefully planned "photo opportunities," he became a symbol of a president "standing tall," one who revitalized myths of leadership and moral authority. Few other American presidents have enjoyed such popularity among the people.

The presidential press conference has become over time an effective symbolic form for the communication of political leadership. Usually at prime television time, America would tune in to a well-publicized session where the President of the United States speaks to reporters in the White House and communicates directly via television to the entire nation. This formal ceremony would then be followed by critiques of the President's remarks by network anchorpersons. By a turn of the TV dial, interested viewers could get further reactions to the news conference from national political commentators.

The Electronic Golden Calf

The presidential press conference has over time become a sensitive barometer of public confidence in government leadership. During the Reagan years it blended a number of elements belonging to traditional ritual occasions. There was a rhythm to the flow of time along with an orderly unfolding of events in a special space. The acknowledged intent of this telecast was to inform the press and the viewing public, but there were implicit functions as well. Camera angles enhanced the drama of the event, offering diverse perspectives: a view from behind the podium, a sweep of the audience of eager reporters, a sharp focus on the questioners as they stood to address the President, a tight shot of the chief executive as he faced and responded to tough questions from a sometimes hostile press. Viewers could thus evaluate the President and observe the way he handled his adversaries. This ritualistic occasion, which featured the charismatic qualities of leadership, was designed to portray a leader in control, ready to meet any situation. Yet in this important political rite Ronald Reagan seemed to falter.

Without a script, unsure of facts, and distanced from some decisions, Reagan frequently resorted to anecdotes. In her book *Eloquence in an Electronic Age*, Kathleen Jamieson has shown how Reagan retreated to storytelling when unable to deal conceptually or factually with questions and issues raised at his press conferences.[15] The president's anecdotal rhetoric, which worked so well in staged photo opportunities and carefully scripted speeches, temporarily enabled him to side-step reporters' questions. He became, nevertheless, increasingly vulnerable before an audience armed with facts and analytical power. Frequently Reagan's misstatements had to be corrected by the White House almost as soon as the conference had

---

[15] Kathleen Hall Jamieson, *Eloquence in an Electronic Age: The Transformation of Political Speechmaking* (New York: Oxford University Press, 1988), pp. 150-151.

ended. His susceptibility to gaffes led his aides to shield him more and more frequently from direct questioning by the press, either formally or informally. Ironically, the Great Communicator had fewer press conferences than any other modern president and was finally insulated almost completely from an open dialogue with the media.

The Legacy of TV Portraiture

Political commentator Roger Mudd has observed that over the eight years of his presidency, Ronald Reagan controlled the public dialogue and set the agenda for issues that would be discussed in the press. His great success as a communicator reinforced the power of the mass media as political tools. Mudd concludes, "Without television, there is no national leadership in the United States anymore." Moreover he asserts that Reagan has set standards for "television presidents" that will be difficult to match. People now expect from their national leaders a TV presence that makes all issues seem "firm, round, fully packed...and bland."[16] Sam Donaldson humorously summed up the image strategy of Reagan aides: "They discovered that an image is worth a thousand facts."[17] Americans found the political portraits especially appealing.

Reagan was attractive for many because of the "good news" posture he brought to the presidency. In explaining his policies—economic, military, social—he and his advisors developed easily recognizable, uncomplicated polarities that work well on TV. Reagan's criticisms of the "naysayers" at the time of the stock market crash showed his disregard of the complexity of the crisis. Still, as he spoke, walking and waving as he left the

---

[16] Roger Mudd, *The MacNeil/Lehrer News Hour*, January 1, 1988.

[17] Sam Donaldson, interview with Hedrick Smith, *The Power Game*, PBS Documentary, Part IV.

The Electronic Golden Calf

White House with Nancy for Camp David, viewers around the world strained to catch his words, intermittently drowned out by the roar of the helicopter blades. And within hours, reactions to these brief telecast images were registered in the stock markets of Tokyo, Hong Kong, and London.

Upbeat and positive, he silhouetted sharply opposed motifs of "we" versus "they": the free world against communism, freedom fighters against totalitarianism, good against evil, reason against madness. The implicit metaphors of warfare are readily symbolic and inspire patriotism. Or, conversely, they may alienate dissenting individuals. Complex presentations with thoughtful qualifications and adjustments had no place in Reagan's political rhetoric; careful thought or scrutiny slowed down the action, and a critical, penetrating look at domestic or foreign policies could be construed as "bad faith." To support his essentially dualistic right/wrong approaches to the thick, intricate problems of human conflict in all spheres of human activity, Ronald Reagan encouraged a state of mind: think positively, keep the faith!

On January 15, 1989, just before the inauguration of President-elect George Bush, Mike Wallace, host of *60 Minutes*, devoted the entire show to an interview with Ronald and Nancy Reagan. You are, he said, leaving the White House as the most popular first couple in a long, long time. The interview began with Mrs. Reagan, and throughout the program many questions were raised about her power and influence on the President. For Ronald Reagan, the program was an opportunity to reiterate his values. Watching this "royal" couple of a technological democratic society recalled for me the sixth-century co-regents, Justinian and Theodora, portrayed on the walls of San Vitale. Separated by centuries and vastly different domains—social, religious, economic, political—their affinity lies in the powerful portrayals of authority crafted with the most sophisticated techniques their cultures afforded.

As Reagan left office, his critics and supporters were unanimous about one thing: he made Americans feel good about themselves. Throughout his presidency, he underscored the traditional values of freedom, family, and patriotism. Both at home and abroad he articulated faith and confidence in the nation and its citizens. While long-range historical assessments of the Reagan presidency are still pending, there is little doubt that the fabrication of political icons to communicate ideology and leadership will continue. The 1988 conventions and presidential campaign underscored their primacy.

Following the conventions, the Republican and Democratic aspirants began the final race for the White House and the campaigns became a battle of symbols and images. Speeches and happenings were orchestrated and assembled in carefully designed sound and sight bytes for the evening news. Thus the media managers in both parties packaged their political products for the networks to offer to the public. A new, post-Reagan George Bush with hard-hitting rhetoric began to master his predecessor's simple antinomies of "right/wrong," "good/liberal," "patriotic/unpatriotic," and they became litanies during the campaign. In the clash of symbols, George Bush was clearly the winner. Much of the success of his campaign can be credited to the design and transformation of his image by his strategists. Standing in the background while a swashbuckling Reagan mesmerized the public, Bush appeared to be a wimpy "yes man." He emerged, however, from his 1988 PR cocoon as a preppy Rambo, charging forth amid unfurled flags, using the same "we" versus "they" slogans that had worked so well for the Great Communicator.

Immediately after his November victory, Bush's media portraitists went to work to sketch another version. The lean, mean, shoot-from-the-hip campaigner was restyled for stately leadership. Adroit brush strokes—film clips of a relaxed family man reaching out a friendly hand to his opponents—covered up

The Electronic Golden Calf

the blemishes of the campaign. The viewing public was introduced to a reflective, kinder, gentler soul, and by the time of Bush's inauguration, the transformation was complete. His address was praised for its balanced, thoughtful comments as well as for its delivery. While a few suggested that he could not compete, in style at least, with the Great Communicator, President Bush presented himself as a thinking man, a man of substance. In the background, symbolism flourished while the White House received its new occupants. The "Gipper" saluted Bush when he and Nancy departed, and the new president saluted back.

Bush inherited many difficult problems. Underpinning them all, however, was the enormous task of separating symbolism from illusion, perhaps from duplicity. He had to assume responsibility for the visual and verbal rhetoric of the campaign, as well as for the symbols of the previous administration with which he became so unmistakably identified. Ceremonial images had to be squared with reality. Bush continually implored voters: "Read my lips...no more taxes." Many recalled that in 1979 those same lips shaped the words "voodoo economics." Even as the Great Communicator praised the family in his farewell address, he submitted a budget that reduced aid to the homeless by fifty percent. Inspiring pictures of the Bush family can only magnify the painful images of families that slipped below the poverty level during the past eight years. Pride in the nation will not, by itself, change America's status as a debtor nation spotted with decaying and drug-ridden cities, a fabulously rich country where over twenty percent of the children are poor. Confidence in ourselves and in the land exist alongside eight years of disregard for conservation and an increasingly polluted earth. The balance between symbol and substance will not be easy for Bush to restore. If this imbalance should not be addressed, the stunning political portraits and patriotic audio-visual hymns to the American Way would become empty ideological propaganda.

Iconifying Public Religion

From TV's political and informational images come popular mythologies and dogmas that represent social norms and expectations. Having observed mythic, informational, and political symbolization in commercial TV, we may ask whether there is an overarching set of beliefs from which these images issue. Can we interpret television as a kaleidoscopic expression of an encompassing faith in the American way of life?

During the several decades of the medium's history, all types of network programming—sports, news, entertainment, commercials, political ceremonies—have collectively formed a mosaic of dynamic images, concrete representations of the economic-social-political system. We have recognized that these symbolic artifacts perform a role like that of the art of previous cultures. Although more fleeting and elusive, TV's electronic images render visible the invisible orders and values of experience. Embodying sentiments and aspirations that transcend denominational loyalties, television has produced symbols of what may be called an American public religion.[18]

---

[18] Since the publication in 1967 of Robert Bellah's seminal article, "Civil Religion in American Society," scholars have examined this concept and the historical reality it sought to describe. Recently James A. Mathiesen has carefully tracked and analyzed those discussions in the context of events in American society. He concludes that an American civil religion reached its peak in 1976 at the time of the Bicentennial and that the academic discussions about it since then have steadily declined. See James A. Mathiesen, "Twenty Years After Bellah: Whatever Happened to Civil Religion?" (Unpublished article) Mathiesen and others point out that the conflicts within the nation—the bitter tensions and debates about Vietnam, disillusionment over Watergate, and the cultural resistance experienced by women and minorities—demonstrate no consensus of faith, religious or otherwise.

The Electronic Golden Calf

Religious sentiments are diffuse and may be dispersed throughout society, even claimed as "truths" by fundamentally different groups. Such sentiments are not confined to a single credal formulation or conceived solely in institutional terms. In *Public Religion in American Culture*, John F. Wilson identifies mythic materials pervasive in American culture. These may be connected with both religious and national identity and appropriated by denominational as well as secular groups. They are shared meanings that "provide frameworks of self-understanding for individual and collective life." These may be better understood, he says, if we examine the many ways in which they become concrete symbols in this richly complex culture.[19]

Wilson's analysis of popular piety and its manifestations provides an excellent foundation for interpreting television's portrayals of faith and values. In a chapter entitled "Religious Meanings of the American Community," he has tried to pin down some of those elusive but deeply ingrained sentiments of faith, sources of piety for an American public religion. These shared meanings he calls "frameworks of intelligibility" operate as if they were religious beliefs. In fact, it might be difficult in a pluralistic culture to distinguish them from religious tenets.

Central to this popular faith are four clusters of meanings, which, Wilson emphasizes, do not exhaust the list that could be compiled. The first reflects faith in national purity, a confidence in "American society understood as perfected and pure, unalloyed and uncompromised. In contrast to the societies of the old world and antiquity, it requires of its members internalized discipline."[20] Some television shows reinforce this sentiment. The concept of an open press conference, for example, represents

---

[19] John F. Wilson, *Public Religion in American Culture* (Philadelphia: Temple University Press, 1979), p. 94.

[20] *Ibid.*, p. 96.

one facet of our faith in America as a pure and uncompromised society. Unattached to either church or state, the press is expected to guard against any deviation from the country's highest aims. If crime and corruption at times appear to dominate local and national TV news, we may blame it on the public taste for horror and sensationalism. At the same time, Americans look to news institutions to play the role of conscience; freedom to do so has traditionally reassured citizens that the earliest visions of this country will not be sullied. Preachers, politicians, and national policies are continually scrutinized—some would say excessively. Television has, nevertheless, been expected to play a watchdog role. Thus TV news coverage can often become the catalyst for people to rethink and reevaluate the nation's adherence to the principles upon which it was founded.

A second elusive tenet of public faith envisions America as the promised land. American society is the "fulfillment of the dreams and aspirations of the ages, frequently exhibited in historical categories and under eschatological symbols, held forth in millenarian language."[21] We recall that in the nineteenth century Thomas Cole used a theological concept to describe this country. America was a land untouched since the time of creation and, unlike the Old World, was destined to open up a distinctly new future for humankind. Less theological but more popular were the Currier and Ives prints that echoed the same theme of a new promised land. Covered wagons were depicted as they made their way through the splendid Rockies. Conquest of indigenous tribes was a darker side of the divine mission: nineteenth-century popular prints that still shame us today show the frontier adventurers and settlers chasing and killing Indians and buffalo as they domesticate and take possession of

---

[21] *Ibid.*

The Electronic Golden Calf

the wilderness. Similarly, TV versions of the fulfillment of these dreams and aspirations of the early settlers have lost many of the theological overtones. We can, nevertheless, discern residual elements in the popular images of cowboys and lawmen depicted in a series like *Gunsmoke*. The God-fearing settlers of *Little House on the Prairie* transform Puritan dreams of a transcendental drama into a more human enterprise in which stalwart families take possession of a new, rich land.

The sense of mission and fulfillment has not been confined to the conquest of the wilderness. It has also been reflected in our explorations in space, where we have assumed that whatever can be technically accomplished should in fact be done. Until the tragedy of the Challenger, our heroes and heroines looked toward the universe for the continuation of our mission. After our "one giant step for mankind" on the moon, there were other distant planets to visit and steps to take. Television drew the American people into these adventures, from liftoff to landing. Meanwhile *Star Trek*, in its past and present versions, continues to satisfy our need for fantasy, aiding our anticipation of an ongoing, special rendezvous in time and space. Without Buck Rogers, Flash Gordon, and *Star Trek*, would Ronald Reagan have successfully marketed his "Star Wars" defense strategy? Have these fictions have become a secularized version of the earlier theological visions of a special people?

Wilson's third "cluster" of meaning centers on "American society as receptive to the deprived and homeless of the world, and promising them new life."[22] While great palaces and churches were being built in Europe, many of the underprivileged left their homelands to make a fresh start in a country where birth and class seemed not to matter. This great myth

---

[22] *Ibid.*

continues to lure the disenfranchised from all parts of the globe to this country. In dramatising that quasi-religious belief, television has been an important medium. Over the last ten years TV has highlighted this country's receptivity to refugees and immigrants who have sought and often found here a second chance in life. On July 4, 1986, we celebrated the refurbishing and hundredth anniversary of the Statue of Liberty. This "lady" was regarded as a fundamental symbol by millions who landed on Ellis Island, from the Irish who had fled the potato famine of the nineteenth century to the most recent refugees from the Middle East. Amid show-biz hype Ronald Reagan flashed a beam that relighted the torch of the Lady of Liberty. Satellite communication made it possible for viewers to witness a naturalization ceremony for 16,000 immigrants in several cities; they saw and heard Chief Justice Warren Burger on Ellis Island lead them in reciting the Pledge of Allegiance.

A fourth source of meaning is our understanding of American society as "one of opportunity in which liberty provides the framework for individual and collective development." This individualist component, Wilson notes, is so obvious and easily assumed that many take it to be the primary root of meaning in American life.[23] The great American dream in both reality and fantasy is the promise of individual growth and development. Such freedom promises a new life, a second chance. It is real to the deprived and homeless who make it to this country either by boat or over the borders. But the same dream is also a fantasy, especially when one compares the mortality rate of infants in Washington, D.C., for example, with that of underdeveloped countries. Still, on television, where mythic themes are emphasized, the aspirations for the good life are often fulfilled.

---

[23] *Ibid.*

The Electronic Golden Calf

The Cosby Show has drawn criticism for its unreality, its artificial and misleading pictures of black family life. Critics claim that the plots are too simple, holding out false hopes, while the portrayal of the Huxtables represents wishful thinking instead of the real situation of black families. Yet Bill Cosby defends his mythological family this way:

> To say that they are not black enough is a denial of the American dream and the American way of life. My point is that this is an American family—an *American* family—and if you want to live like they do, and you're willing to work, the opportunity is there.[24]

Here Cosby is standing fast by the dream itself, a dogmatic, enduring sentiment that *any* person—black, white, or whatever—can make it in this society with a lot of hard work and some luck. The show is mythological in its promises of a new life and an opportunity for individual growth and development. Supporters argue, moreover, that it presents a much-needed counter-image for negative stereotypes. But the dominant themes sounded by Cosby are that the family is central and that America is a place where the promise of new life is indeed real.

The new, improved, good life for most Americans—whatever their race, creed, or social status—is preeminently centered upon the notion of "choice." "Choice" is, in fact, the most magical word in American culture. It is an inclusive word, applied indiscriminately to decisions important and trivial, ranging from a marriage partner to a deodorant. The steady hum over radio and television about the choices we have is a litany to liberty, to the freedom to choose one product over another, and above all

---

[24] Richard Zogin, reported by Scott Brown, Dan Godgame, and Jeannie Ralston, "Cosby, Inc.," *Time* (September 28, 1987), p. 60.

to define one's individuality through one's choices. Throughout the vast network of advertising and entertainment one of the fundamental American dogmas of public religion—liberty—has been homogenized to fit both banal and profound moments of will. Deliberation and the will to act have been contained and domesticated. A choice of soap powder readily takes its place alongside the selection of a political candidate. In a sense advertising has become a caricature of liberty, as it emphasizes buying and selling and neglects the more profound dimensions of personal freedom.

John Wilson stresses that these clusters of meaning do not exhaust the beliefs of an American public religion, but they are central to an underlying popular piety in American society. Moreover, these meanings and symbols manifest themselves not in any one single community, but in patriotic societies and lodges, veterans and regional groups, and civic clubs—voluntary organizations that characterize our collective life. And on special occasions such as Memorial Day or the Fourth of July, "the true believers symbolically display the roles they believe that they bear for the whole community throughout the year."[25] Even though there may be tensions between such groups and traditional religious denominations, common to all is the conviction that American society and its democratic principles deserve our final loyalty. Throughout the culture there is a primordial attachment to these quasi-religious tenets—in business, merchandising, entertainment, sports, and religious denominations.

Adapting Wilson's insights to television, we see that the piety and symbols of an American public religion are not confined to a particular type of program. Instead, symbols are selec-

---

[25] Wilson, *Public Religion in American Culture*, p. 142. See especially Chapter 6, "Social Institutions and American Public Religion."

The Electronic Golden Calf

tively chosen and infused into programs of many kinds. Collectively they merge and work together to form a composite montage of the values we associate with the American Way.

The Iconofiers

The construction of symbols that embody the faith of an American public religion parallels the processes of earlier religious art where, under the auspices of church and state, small, powerful groups devised subject matter and empowered skilled artisans to produce images that would reinforce belief. In his essay "Art and Society," Kenneth Clark argued that a "healthy" relationship existed when the elite patrons and craftsmen fashioned symbols which the majority embraced and honored as their own.[26] The complex portals and stained glass windows of medieval churches, for example, came about through the combined efforts of two very specialized classes of people. Educated clergy and theologians worked out elaborate iconographical programs, drawing upon tradition as well as their own learning and imagination. Mastercraftsmen—stone, glass, and metal workers—equally skilled and imaginative in their own arts, took these theological schemes and gave them concrete form. The combined inventiveness of both groups is reflected in churches such as Vézelay and Chartres. When townspeople and peasants saw these as embodiments of their faith, "art" was fulfilling its prime sacramental function: giving tangible, visible expression to beliefs and values with which ordinary people could identify. Clark, of course, was taking his material largely from ancient and medieval times. His description, nevertheless, could be transposed and applied to current television and its promulgation of an American public religion.

---

[26] Clark, "Art and Society," pp. 62-64.

Today diverse special groups—corporate sponsors, ad agencies, network executives—agree upon the basic themes and motifs and authorize other groups of gifted writers, artists, and production teams to create symbols to appeal to the public. Like their ancient and medieval counterparts, these symbol-makers attempt to strike a responsive chord in the hearts and minds of believers. "Believing" in this case, is no longer tied to traditional religions but to something we vaguely perceive as the American way.

Today the formulation and refinement of sacramental images is often based on testing and analysis of consumer interests. Advertising and marketing firms have long used focus groups to try to determine the symbolic content of their ads. Bringing together individuals with common tastes, they observe the responses of certain types of consumers or voters. They try out catchy phrases, images, or ideas and measure the reactions they trigger. Media expert Richard Wirthlin has described how he used a "speech pulse" mechanism to identify phrases in Ronald Reagan's speeches that drew the most positive responses. Holding small gadgets in their hands, the subjects could press the gadget to indicate their reactions. Rising pulses indicated phrases that appealed to the listeners. These were communicated to speech writers and designated phrases would be recycled in speech after speech.[27] When research of this kind is combined with the work of pollsters, copywriters, and camera crews, we have an elite corps working together to develop the symbols that ordinary people may embrace.

A number of critics are beginning to warn that the democratic principles of liberty and choice are eroding under the onslaught of TV's synthetic rituals and icons. Some have

---

[27] Hedrick Smith, "The Power Game," PBS Documentary, Part IV.

The Electronic Golden Calf

spoken out about the marketing approach to politics. Still others point to the formation of giant economic conglomerates that threaten the diversity of the media.

"You begin to feel you are responsible for the direction of America," says media consultant Charles Guggenheim. "Even if it's true, I don't think one should feel particularly good about it." Before he got out of political advertising, Guggenheim created ads for liberals and conservatives, Republicans and Democrats, including Adlai Stevenson, the Kennedys, Arkansas Governor Orville Faubus, and Missouri Senator John Danforth. Guggenheim points out that the scale of political TV declined from thirty-minute films to five minutes and finally to sixty and thirty-second spots. He attributes the staccato timing not just to politicians, but to networks concerned with money and prime-time ratings. The shorter ads are especially suitable to superficial, negative messages, but as the Bush campaign showed, they work. Neither the politicians nor their constituencies are apt to change them. "There's nothing in the Constitution or in federal law that says the process should be carried out in sixty seconds. We just accept it."[28]

Finally, there are critics who warn that the threat to the democratic principles of the American Way is formidable and cannot be grasped simply by critiquing the work of media managers and journalists. Ben Bagdikian has pointed out in *Media Monopoly* the concentration of power which has been building as the diverse ownership of media corporations declines. In 1982, in Bagdikian's first studies, he found that half or more of all media in the United States were controlled by fifty corporations. The revised edition of his book in 1986 indicated that the fifty had dropped to twenty-nine; his later studies indi-

---

[28] Jonathan Rowe, "Media Mogul Bows Out of the Political Ad Game," *The Christian Science Monitor* (November 29, 1988), p. 4.

cated a further drop, in 1987, to twenty-six. Citing Wall Street predictions, Bagdikian warns that in the 1990s as few as six companies may control all media.

He also points out that as print and electronic communications depend increasingly on advertising, the opportunity for pluralism and the separation of interests may diminish even more:

> Mass advertising is no longer solely a means of introducing and distributing consumer goods, though it does that. It is a major mechanism in the ability of a relatively small number of giant corporations to hold disproportionate power over the economy. These corporations need newspapers, magazines, and broadcasting not just to sell their goods but to maintain their economic and political influence....And increasingly they are not only needed by but owned by the corporate giants.[29]

Print and electronic media are not neutral agents displaying consumer goods, but vital instruments of power for major corporations. For Bagdikian and other critics the question is one of genuine freedom: How can the media in America perform their traditional role of an open, truly free mediator among all the forces in society when they have beome an integral part of one?

If we are moving steadily toward a media monopoly, the consequences are enormous. We are accustomed to monopolies and to unforeseen natural disasters that affect the flow of oil or determine the price of sugar, coffee, or grain. But we have not fully grasped the implication of the exclusive shaping and control of the information market, especially in the United States, where most people expect the press to be genuinely free to oversee democratic processes.

---

[29] Ben H. Bagdikian, *The Media Monopoly* (Boston: Beacon, 1983), p. 152. See alson Bagdikian's article, "The Lords of the Global Village," *The Nation* (June 12, 1989).

The Electronic Golden Calf

In this chapter I have explored some ways in which the technological revolution of mass media in the United States has also been a *sacramental revolution*, whereby easily understood images give concrete expression to invisible ideals. To me the most important question for artists and designers is this: How do these images function in a democratic, technological, and secular world? In addressing that question I have tried to show that our society, like others, uses images to construct symbolic worlds which represent beliefs and values.

The high arts today no longer play a significant role in expressing shared public values and myths. Indeed, most people expect artists to present personal mythologies and private visions. On the other hand the public communication of myths, a function of high art in earlier centuries, during the twentieth century has been increasingly taken over by popular culture. Today the mass media offer the public a bewildering array of symbolic worlds and myths which purport to explain and order experience.

Various kinds of institutions in American culture—political, informational, economic, and religious—have tapped the sacramental power of the media; they develop symbolic worlds to generate and encourage a sense of identity and loyalty. In this enterprise TV myths and rituals may often represent superficial, even distorted world views. Unless we recognize the power of the media to construct symbolic worlds, we will not even grasp the range of mediated values or recognize the real choices to be made. Nor will we understand the need for a daring iconoclasm. We will simply stay tuned in. If we do not closely evaluate the mythic power of mass communications, we risk becoming prisoners of illusion—like those in Plato's parable who, in seeing and naming shadows cast on the wall, believed that they understood themselves and all reality.

Some Americans may look to religious institutions for help in sorting out multiple layers of signs and symbols that overlay their lives. But do church congregations seriously consider the roles that the visual arts now play in contemporary culture? High art has become for many artists a spiritual pilgrimage; for museum devotees and investors, the work of art is an object of meditation or treasured commodity. At the same time, the images of popular art permeate culture, enlivening it with civic rituals and easily understood icons. In a society saturated with symbols, do churches and synagogues distinguish their own? Are these at all vital in an image-driven secular society?

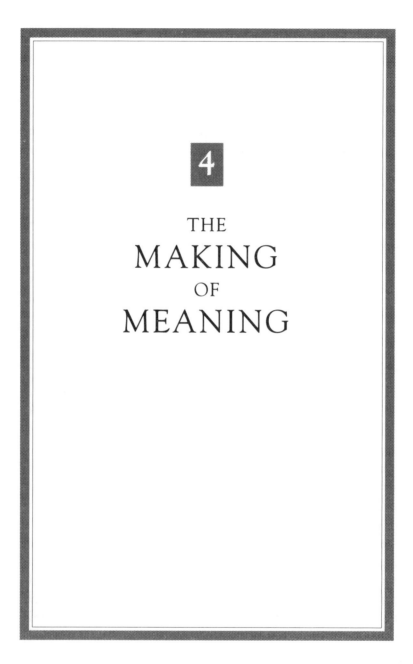

4

THE
MAKING
OF
MEANING

f the high arts today convey private visions and myths, while the popular arts have taken over the communication of public values and meanings, what is left for religion? What vital images can the church and synagogue put forward? People enter the great medieval devotional centers of Europe, such as those at Chartres and Vézelay, as they would a museum, while modern religious art seems to them hopelessly irrelevant. Can the mainline churches do anything with the popular arts, such as TV? Can churches and synagogues appropriate high art in any way? Does it have a place in sacred spaces? In this last chapter I want to consider some of the challenges that both high and popular culture have presented to religious groups in the late twentieth century.

We associate the autonomy of art with cultural developments of the last hundred years, yet its independence is only one facet of modernity. The visual arts over time have acquired not only independence from institutional religion, but also two roles once associated with it.

The primary, essential role shared by world religions is a redemptive one. In various ways they all offer salvation, a way out of human suffering and meaninglessness. Each provides a process or path—prayers, rites, meditations, rituals—through which individuals sustain a lifelong journey of faith toward an end which is ultimately a mystery. As societies became increasingly secularized, this fundamental function of religion has been fractured and fragmented into paths of salvation distinct from traditional ones. In the nineteenth century, and especially during the twentieth, the pursuit of art has been transformed into a spiritual pilgrimage.

The Making of Meaning

Discontented with institutional religion, a number of twen-tieth-century artists have found in the practice of art a way of faith and reflection. As we saw earlier, painters Kandinsky and Mondrian explored the life of the spirit through their art and believed that the forms they created could awaken and inspire spirituality in others. Mid-century abstractionists such as Rothko and Newman also expected their works to be for viewers, as they were for the artists themselves, sources for med-itation. Students in art schools today, especially in the fine arts, frequently see their commitment to art as a contemplative, ex-ploratory journey. In this chapter we want to ask why the arts have become a means of individual religious exploration and to consider how traditional religious communities—churches and synagogues—may use this challenge to reexamine and revitalize their own historical sacramental forms.

In contrast to high art, popular images today perform a legiti-mating function in American society and also fulfill a more in-direct role that religion once played. Even today, in compact societies where religious communities still confer or reinforce a sense of identity, religion performs a confirming and integrative part. In addition to its manifest, saving dimension, traditional religion has always offered an account of reality which enabled individuals and groups to place themselves in a social as well as an eternal scheme of things. In advanced, pluralistic societies, however, this latent role of religion has been taken over by other authorities—political, economic, and scientific—which provide their constituencies with information, values, and iden-tities.

In the United States, however, the mass media have become extraordinarily powerful in their capacity to legitimate certain basic American values and convictions. While most of us are thinking in the categories furnished by *TV Guide*, there is a deep level of symbolization which *all* programs collectively form. What we see and hear, without reflection, appear to be images of our world. Actually they make up a huge canopy of fabricated audio-visual signs which serve as common references for millions of Americans. Thus television images, particularly in the United States, are public, shared symbols that for many Americans answer the questions "Who am I?" and "Who are we?" Under this giant canopy of images all denominations and religious traditions are exposed to the same framing of reality.

A similar frame of reality was achieved in ancient and medieval art. Earlier we considered the classical aesthetic and its figurative visual language which narrated popular myths on the pediments and friezes of temples and other public buildings. While we may enshrine fragments of these sculpted forms and celebrate them today as "high art," they were, nevertheless, the popular legitimating and integrative images at the time they were created. Sponsored by political and clerical authorities, they were expected to communicate to ordinary, unlettered people their history and values.

Climbing to the Acropolis, an Athenian citizen could stand at the base of the Parthenon and, looking up, see the images that identified common loyalties. Depicted on the frieze, for example, was the ceremonial event which honored the patron goddess Athena. Presented in relief sculpture were Athenian citizens who formed a procession and made their way through the city and up the sacred way to the temple and the statue of the goddess. The figures and faces of the marble reliefs are perfectly executed in noble, heroic dimensions. But was this the "reality" of fifth-century Athens? Not according to Thucydides, Socrates, Plato, and the Sophists. Below in the streets of Athens, life was raw and ugly, difficult to transcend. A portion of a Sophist fragment reads: "Life, even when it is happy, has nothing great or noble, but in reality is petty, feeble, short-lived and mixed with sorrow." Images from the Parthenon do not portray the fragility and sorrow of ordinary experience, but rather

The Making of Meaning

the myths and ceremonies that bestowed identity upon a people.

Today our friezes, the visual narratives of grandeur and perfection, may be found in popular art. Our mythological dramas, heroes and heroines, and ideological visions are produced through the contemporary forms of soap operas, sit-coms, commercials, news and sports. Like the sculpted images on ancient and medieval architecture, the figures created by electronic impulses also portray values and ideologies; similarly, they may be as remote from everyday life as were the earlier idealized pictures of ordinary men and women. Although separated by centuries of symbolic and technological revolutions, the beautiful people depicted on the Parthenon frieze and those represented in TV commercials are comparably value-laden. In both instances the visual images assist in performing the latent, legitimating role of religion: the framing of "reality," the shaping of a commonly understood world.

During the twentieth century high and popular art have played different, complementary roles once associated with traditional religion. But the dominant religion in the United States today is an invisible one, "a symbolic universe" enlivened by faith in the American Way.[1] Within this symbolic ambience each of these two spheres of the visual arts has challenged the religious imagination, although in quite different ways. In this chapter I want to look at the nature of both challenges, beginning with those of popular art, particularly television.

---

[1] See Peter L. Berger and Thomas Luckmann, *The Social Construction of Reality* (Garden City, NY: Doubleday, 1967), pp. 95-96.

The Symbolic Canopy

The symbols of an American public religion radiate throughout the culture. Through television and other popular arts the nation is blanketed with mythic, informational, and political images. Do churches and synagogues today emphasize the distinctiveness of their own symbols which hover beneath this encompassing canopy? Or have their symbols become fused with the pervasive myths and civic rituals perpetuated through popular culture?

Responses to these questions will undoubtedly vary, depending upon individual and group concerns, age and educational levels, political, economic, and ethnic factors, as well as liturgical practices. Complicating these and other variables is the sheer difficulty of interpreting visual forms. As media professionals understand, images communicate in ways that words do not. It has been shown that people often remember TV pictures, but forget the reporting or narratives broadcast with them. We also know that television commercials are consciously designed and constructed, but as researchers point out, individual responses to them are often ambiguous and subjective. Given the wide range of interpretation, the evaluation and analysis of TV symbolism is most productive when it takes place in groups where people may collectively sort out their responses and attitudes. Later on I want to suggest issues which particular congregations can explore, because an awareness of TV's symbolic canopy becomes clearer when groups consider their own loyalties and values alongside those of public religion.

Robert Wuthnow, a sociologist who has extensively analyzed American religious groups, has pointed out that conservative civil religion is more closely identified with a biblical faith which claims a special place for this country in the divine order of things, while a liberal view focuses less on the nation and more on humanity. "Rather than drawing specific attention to the distinctiveness of the Judeo-Christian tradition," Wuthnow

The Making of Meaning

points out, "liberal civil religion is much more likely to include arguments about basic human rights and common human problems."[2] Typical concerns would be nuclear disarmament, human rights, world hunger, peace and justice. Liberal civil religionists differ from secularists or humanists in their emphasis upon faith and their identification with the biblical prophetic tradition. Wuthnow's findings can be very useful in identifying certain types of attitudes toward prevailing cultural symbols, as well as toward the television medium itself. In the light of his research we may ask: How have religious conservatives used the TV medium to put forth their message and beliefs? How have religious liberals used television to promote their causes? What cultural symbols do these different constituencies resist or embrace?

Regardless of denomination, religious conservatives have found TV useful in communicating their gospel. Jerry Falwell's regular telecast broadcasts from the Thomas Road Baptist Church in Lynchburg, Virginia typify conservative attempts to use the medium for expressing the Christian principles he espouses. In Falwell's program "The Old-Time Gospel Hour," television techniques are used to modify and visually enhance the formal elements of a free church, evangelical service. Television cameras provide a variety of angles and detailed shots to give the viewer the sense of being present in a sacred space. The central lectern is flanked by flowers, and Falwell stands behind it as he reads or preaches. Although he usually wears a dark business suit, the choir behind him is robed. When he reads from the Bible a camera films the page, and printed passages appear and fill the viewer's screen. Other modifications depend entirely upon the medium. For example, in the middle of a sermon an il-

---

2   Robert Wuthnow, *The Restructuring of American Religion* (Princeton, NJ: Princeton University Press), p. 250.

lustration or extension of Falwell's message is made by inserting a taped interview he has previously prepared.

Frequently Falwell's sermons address national issues—social, economic, and political. And even though they conclude with the invitation to come forward and profess one's faith, he also exhorts viewers to take a stand for public policies he is advocating, such as the right-to-life movement. This flexibility of emphasis suggests a shift in the function of these televised worship services. Nationally broadcast interpretations of views on social issues suggest an educational rather than liturgical function. While instruction cannot be separated from the evangelist's call for repentance, Falwell's advocacy for causes plays an equally important role. Television transforms a sacramental occasion into an opportunity to advocate socio-political causes from a religiously conservative point of view.

The program created by Pat Robertson, *The 700 Club*, also illustrates how television can be used to promulgate a conservative civil religion. Among the video evangelists he has developed the most complex type of programming, with features styled after those of commercial television. At *The 700 Club* there is no traditional sacred space such as the ones used by Jerry Falwell, Robert Schuller, and others. The program is broken down into segments as diverse as talk-show routines and cooking adventures modeled after those of Julia Child. The studio space itself resembles a posh library in an upper-middle-class home, with natural wood paneling, while guests on the show include successful business men and women, politicians, and ordinary people who have had extraordinary religious experiences. Their common denominator is generally their testimony to the power of God in their lives as they struggle upward in this great nation. Robertson, a law school graduate, occasionally goes into a detailed analysis of news events or political concerns. Standing before a huge world map, he discusses a particular global crisis and then meanders on to biblical and

The Making of Meaning

theological themes, speculating about its significance for biblical prophecy, especially in the Middle East.

Liberal religious groups have not systematically developed TV communication as extensively as more conservative organizations; mainline denominations have generally been more cautious about the medium than evangelicals. Moreover, many mainline groups, unlike evangelicals, have for many years been given free time—first on radio and later on television—to broadcast their formal worship services. In many cities stations still offer air time to some churches and synagogues, although often in undesirable time slots. Advocates of liberal religious views have depended more upon national news coverage and critical journalism in documentaries.

The cause of religious liberals of the 1960s, for example, was advanced through the camerawork of TV journalists who covered the freedom marches in the South. Scenes of the marchers attacked by police with fire hoses and dogs were telecast throughout the nation; these images vividly proclaimed the cause of the clergy who had rallied behind Martin Luther King, Jr. This coverage was typical, for without massive funding for television production, liberal groups have only one option: to get their causes before the public through the nightly news. This option continues to be used by religious liberals to direct the attention of the nation to issues such as human rights and the plight of the homeless.

The documentary tradition of photo-journalists and filmmakers has consistently been used in television to highlight what religious liberals see as fundamental ethical issues. Documentaries have been produced by commercial networks, independent producers, PBS, and occasionally by religious groups. One example is the provocative program of Bill Moyers' "People Like Us," in 1984, which focused on the extreme hardship of disabled persons who had been taken off welfare during the Reagan administration. Liberal public religionists welcome the appearance of this kind of critical, ethical imperative in the main-stream of everyday programming. Documentaries, however, are not seen by many viewers, and therefore do not receive the high ratings scored by top network shows; very often, even after a sequence of documentaries dealing with particular social issues, the problems remain unsolved.

In the early 1980s an independent film-maker, Anna Carrigan, produced a documentary that sensitized many Americans to the agonizing conflicts in Central America. "Roses in December" was widely acclaimed for its artistic and prophetic power and appeared on public television. The film told the story of four American churchwomen murdered in San Salvador in 1980. Three members of religious orders—two Maryknoll, one Ursuline—and a lay worker were senselessly killed by National Guardsmen associated with the right wing military. Eventually the five guardsmen were caught and given thirty-year sentences for their crime. Later, various constituencies of the Roman Catholic Church combined resources to make a Hollywood film based on the life of Archbishop Romero, assassinated in 1980. Produced by Elwood E. Kieser, a Paulist priest, the film details the last three years of Romero's life and his defense of human rights in the Salvadoran civil war. Hoping to portray an inspirational yet fully human leader, producer Kieser summarizes their realistic depiction of Archbishop Romero: "Here is a man who was flawed, who was dragged kicking and screaming into heroism, but who finally surrendered his life to God and let God speak and act through him."[3]

During the 1980's the Maryknoll order began to produce distinctive films which focused on the social concerns of the church throughout the world. Several of their documentaries

---

[3] Larry Rohter, "'Romero' Finds A Producer: The Church," *New York Times* (November 13, 1988), p. 13.

The Making of Meaning

gained critical attention. "Consuming Hunger" was selected among competing productions by Nova and the commercial networks to receive the World Hunger Media Award, 1988-89. It also received the silver medal in the New York International Film and Video Festival, as well as a blue ribbon in the American Film and Video Festival. An earlier film, "Gods of Metal," which dealt with the arms race from a Christian perspective, framed the moral issues facing the world community and documented the effects of the arms race on the poor in the United States and overseas. This film was nominated for an Academy Award.

Thus far I have tried to indicate how particular loyalties to the religious right or left favor certain uses and forms of television. The underlying assumption of the previous chapter, however, was that commercial television as it developed over the decades tended to embody an overarching faith in an American public religion, hovering above the denominations and avoiding the extreme ideologies of right or left. Again Wuthnow's study is helpful. He points out that the liberal/conservative tensions among denominations and civil religionists have turned many people off, allowing secular ideology to play a more prominent legitimating role in American society. One of the most frequently voiced principles used to reinforce belief and distinguish national loyalty is the value of "freedom." Readily appropriated by many groups, the dogma of freedom may be invoked to justify all kinds of political, social, and economic interests. It can be used to advance an outrageous materialism as well as explain a commitment to asceticism. Citing opinion polls, Wuthnow indicates that Americans believe there is a close relationship between their freedom and the free enterprise system. This overarching myth of freedom, he says, is empowered by its intangibility and by its reinforcement of the common belief that "we are in charge of our own lives, and therefore, are morally accountable for what we do."[4]

Television in particular has played an important role in perpetuating and celebrating this guiding principle of the American Way. The heroes and heroines of television—in sports, news, sitcoms, soaps—achieve distinction as they take charge of their destiny. Diverse personalities—from Mary Tyler Moore and Matt Dillon to J.R. Ewing, Alex Keaton, and Roseanne Barr—personify the exercise of freedom in choosing and creating their lifestyles. Most important, the print and electronic media together have formed a zone of thought comparable to the atmosphere in which we breathe and move. The encompassing environment of images and sound—radio, televison, magazines, and newspapers—produces creatures who discover their freedom as they choose and consume. Freedom and responsibility as citizens are exercised by buying objects which enhance us as individuals and help to maintain society's growth. Such actions are transformed by advertising into assertions of faith in the larger political-economic system.

Even though popular culture has tended to trivialize the profound dimensions of freedom in a democracy, it has in its own way broadcast this value into distant and vastly different cultures. Coke and Pepsi ads and re-runs of *Gunsmoke, I Love Lucy,* and *Dallas* have witnessed throughout the world to a way of life and celebrated the freedom of individuals to exercise choice, to take charge of their lives. During 1988 and 1989 the idea of individual liberty associated with western democracies was forcefully animated in distant places by surging throngs of Chinese students in Beijing. In November of 1989 the Berlin wall was effectively toppled as eastern and western Berliners were allowed

---

4 Wuthnow, *The Restructuring of American Religion*, pp. 259, 262.

The Making of Meaning

to move freely across this historical barrier. Some crossed over to begin new lives in West Berlin; others came to shop and to see relatives and friends. American anchormen rushed there to report the occasion, and TV viewers worldwide vicariously danced with those on top of the wall. Reflecting later upon the event, freelance journalist Hedrick Smith described those he'd seen who began to "breathe the air of freedom." Georgie Anne Geyer, journalist for the Universal Press Syndicated, connected this historic moment with the information revolution which has been under way for at least the last ten years. West German television, she observed, has been going over the wall "like birds migrating." TV couldn't be stopped; East Germans could see what was happening in the West.[5]

The capacity of television to communicate both verbally and visually makes it a powerful tool for promoting both secular and religious ideologies. Thus we need to ask how various, even competing faiths, appropriate television for their own ends. Are there technical aspects of television which are particularly effective in the communicating of religious faith, broadly conceived as the human need for meaning—the drive to make sense of life?

Persuasive Imaging

In their use of TV there are at least four points at which liberal and conservative denominations, as well as political or secular faiths, converge. These are the importance of charismatic leadership, polarization of belief, conversion, and sacramentalism. In each of these areas television has transformed older forms of communication through its imagistic revolution.

---

[5]   *Washington Week in Review*, November 10, 1989.

Persuasive rhetoric by gifted religious and political leaders is nothing new. Ancient myths abound with stories of heroes and demi-gods with extraordinary gifts, and today all of us can point to persons who inspire trust and lead others. Found in all walks of life, they are teachers, saints, athletes, salesmen, soldiers, and newscasters. In the United States, however, where television has become a major source of authority, charisma in leaders has become essential in marshalling and influencing public opinion. In the past a charismatic leader might have influenced a local cult, religious order, military or political unit. Television has, however, altered the extent of the influence and power of persuasive individuals—especially in religion and politics. It is hard to imagine how, without television, evangelical preachers could have built their empires or how a movie star could so easily have gained landslide political victories.

Television is especially compatible with those religious traditions that have emphasized the charismatic qualities of leadership and played down the office of the priesthood and the saving role of the sacraments. Sacral power becomes concentrated in the person who has been divinely called to teach, preach, and heal; television offers an unprecedented opportunity to focus on the personality and forcefulness of religious leaders. Fulton J. Sheen, Martin Luther King, Jr., Billy Graham, Jesse Jackson, and Pat Robertson have all been beneficiaries of TV technology. Their preaching, prophecy, teaching, and healing took on dimensions of "real life" for millions of viewers. Much of their success depends upon special qualities of body, mind, and spirit, seen and immediately felt. Television techniques can intensify their zeal and bring viewers into intimate contact. We are all familiar with the eyeball-to-eyeball images provided by a zoom lens: the fiery or tear-filled eyes, the intensity of prayer and supplication. Such close engagement with charismatic leaders, shared by thousands at the same moment, is possible only through the medium of television.

The Making of Meaning

A second point of convergence is the polarization of ideological positions into easily understood right/wrong formulae for
mass audiences. The formal dynamics of the medium—evident
in both religious and commercial television—seem to draw its
users into an inevitable over-simplification and even caricatur-
ing of issues. The strength and attraction of television is its
brisk, flashy pace. As a result of both its form and style, the
commercial has had a "trickle down" effect on our expectations
of news as well as on other types of programming. In the context
of American broadcasting, the black or white, right or wrong
positions work best; shades of gray seem dull or too complicated
to watch. Thus politicians and preachers tend to draw hard, fast
lines between good and evil, to simplify complex human problems—social, political, economic, or religious—and they speak
without qualification of what is "American," "biblical," or
"Christian."

Religious and political groups, whether liberal or conservative, understand what best suits the medium of television. Metaphors of warfare and struggle, the conflict with satanic forces,
and the urgency to locate the enemy are applied to tensions and
problems of the moral life, for both the individual and society.
Would the agonizing civil wars in Central America have gone
on for such a long time without the over-simplification by
American politicians? Ronald Reagan and Oliver North saw the
contras as freedom fighters keeping the communists from the
borders of south Texas. To others they were "terrorists," rem-
nants of the Somoza regime, who bullied and tortured civilians
who would not aid them. Introspective reflection, ambiguities,
exhausting shades of gray, and the multiple interconnectedness
of human evil are usually not compatible with television timing,
show business or video technology. A Manichean principle of
easily divisible and discernible forces works far better in evoking
fundamentalist fervor among viewers. Politician Ronald Reagan
and his advisors understood how to frame moral choices in the

simplest terms. Thus whenever the public and Congress seemed to become bogged down in the complexities of the Latin American struggles or waver in their complete support of the contras, the Great Communicator went to the television pulpit. From the Oval Office he repeated his homily on democracy versus communism and urged the audience to make clear moral decisions and write their congressional representatives.

The use of television to exhort viewers to take action represents a third intersection of secular and religious broadcasting. Politicians, evangelists, and creators of commercials all seek the same thing: conversion, or *metanoia*, the "turning around" of viewers. The revivalist format, with its emphasis upon conversion, is ideally suited to television. William McLoughlin, scholar of American religion, has shown how the series of great awakenings in this country, with their large mass tent meetings may be seen as prototypes of what we now call media events.[6] Today residual elements of the conversionist principle can be found in many types of TV communication. Charismatic personalities, whose special gifts of body and spirit work a kind of magic over the airwaves, transform the television scene into a generic sacred space where altar calls can take place in various forms: in commercials, political speeches, or televised religious services.

Although electronic preachers and politicians work in different spaces—the church itself, a talk-show studio, a large auditorium or arena, or frequencies on which political sound bytes are aired on the nightly news—the conversion principle plays a dominant role. Common to all is a fervent appeal to individuals to make a decision, a profession of faith. In some cases, testimonials and confessions are punctuated by preaching, informal

---

6 William McLoughlin, *Revivals, Awakening and Reform: An Essay on Religion and Social Change in America, 1607-1977* (Chicago: University of Chicago Press, 1978), p. 208.

173

The Making of Meaning

talking, or interpreting world events. All insist that central to faith and practice is a decisive change of heart. Contemporary electronic preachers have used the media to underscore a type of religious experience deeply rooted in one type of Protestantism in America. The video evangelists, who regard conversion as a key to salvation and a radical turning point in the life of the individual, construct their messages around that central principle.

The most condensed format of the conversionist motif is the TV commercial, which has become essential to both network and religious broadcasting. Embedded in its structure are sentiments from our religious and political heritage: salvation and choice. Newness of life can now be associated with a change of heart about politics, the purchase of a new car, or the selection of a beverage. A Pepsi commercial, for example, designed to fit the charismatic personality and gifts of singer Michael Jackson, became an invitation to make a decision and join in. Images and sounds of the soft-drink ad drew viewers into a growing throng of happy, dancing people following the steps of a dynamic cultural hero. Even couch potatoes might have been roused, vicariously at least, to skip lightly behind the agile Jackson as he led his ecstatic followers to the right choice. The conversionist call in this instance is to come on up to the good life through Pepsi. Nonetheless, it plays upon the persuasive motifs of turning around and becoming a part of something larger. The psychological state of mind that William James and A.D. Nock attributed to a transforming experience—that clean and beautiful newness within and without, the removal of anxiety, and the surge of ecstasy and confidence—begins to sound like generic copy for use by preacher, politician, artist, or ad writer. The phenomenon once viewed as intrinsically religious now seems to be flourishing in a secular, consumer society.

Finally, we want to look at what might be described as a technological sacramentalism. As in ancient and medieval times, people today seem to depend upon some concrete, material expression which confirms or nurtures their sense of belonging—some tangible form of contact with authority and power. This need may be satisfied by the reassuring image and voice of a politician, preacher, or anchor person. However superficial and impersonal these images are, they are nevertheless a palpable link to a comforting leader. Televangelists were quick to understand the importance of this sustained contact, and modern technology offers many new types of devotional forms— along with innumerable books, pamphlets, charts, and pins that are continually mailed out to loyal viewers. Traditional holy cards and icons have been updated by plastic, decorator colors, and stereophonic headphones that attune the devout to video cassette sermons and spirituals. Icons of tradition, their "magic" now sanitized and rationalized, have become acceptable forms of sacramentalism, sanctified by technology.

More than other evangelists, Jim Bakker sensed the human need for tangible symbols of faith and turned it into big business. In an uncanny way this evangelical preacher exploited an age-old desire to move out of ordinary routines and spaces and to seek the spiritual through a pilgrimage to the extraordinary. Like other pilgrims in search of sacred sites and holy relics, modern middle-class devotees made their way to Heritage USA. At Bakker's spiritual-recreational center in South Carolina they found both entertainment and a symbolic environment to nurture both religious and national piety. This modern-day sacred site featured baptisms, healing, and Bible study along with sumptuous dining, entertainment, and of course, shopping. Just before the Bakkers' sudden departure in 1986, it had become the third most popular theme park in America.

In the midst of bubbling hotel fountains, ice cream parlors, boutiques, and prayer sessions, distinctions between the sacred and the secular were blurred. Did Bakker know of similar mixtures in ancient and medieval sacred sites? Was it his attach-

The Making of Meaning

ment to material values or some insight about the blend of the physical and spiritual? Or did the Bakkers simply manipulate TV's persuasive power and obliterate all distinctions between religion and culture?

The blurring of the distinctive values of religion and culture is neither new nor unique, and in the past it has often sparked religious reforms or rejection of certain art forms. Considering the ways in which secular and religious motifs often become intertwined in television, it is not suprising that many persons deny that the medium can address the deepest human needs or meaning, or sustain thoughtful reflection. Some even argue that TV is a malevolent force and should be altogether rejected. Still others believe that all cultural forms, including television, can be redemptively transformed and reappropriated for the good of both individuals and society.

Rejection or Transformation?

We may recall that the earliest response of Christians to the prevailing culture, including its forms of communication, was one of rejection. In a similar way some persons today oppose using the popular arts to communicate religious sentiments, while many are outraged at the thought of any endorsement of television. Many critics see television as a corrupting influence and some have explained in elaborate detail the harmfulness of the medium and why it must simply be thrown out. Malcolm Muggeridge, a critic concerned with TV's harmful effect upon spirituality and sensibility, has labeled it a "fantasy machine." Contemporary mass media and especially television, says Muggeridge, have forged a powerful brainwashing operation which is eroding traditional values. The media lure us into a fantasy world which conflicts with the "reality of our existence as made in the image of God."[7] Moreover, television promotes a cult of consumerism by appealing to our cupidity and vanity, and it evokes and appeals to our most appetitive tendencies.

By treating television as something inherently destructive, something to avoid and, if possible, eliminate from our lives, such critics recall the ideas of one of the earliest Christian commentators upon culture, Tertullian. This stalwart church father warned Christians against the defilements of pagan society— from cosmetics to images to warfare. Many persons today believe that the only answer to the challenge of mass communications, and especially television, is a similar rejection. For in a free society, one need not tune in or even own a television set. If there is only one view of the world created by television programs, we can choose to be unaware of it. Yet even the forceful critic Muggeridge qualifies his position somewhat in the last essay of *Christ and the Media*. While continually reiterating his position that television manufactures contemporary fantasy, he asks, "Does this mean that the camera and all its works are wholly evil and incapable of fulfilling God's purposes? Of course not."[8] As in all human creations, there are elements of the media which may be redemptive and life-enriching. He cites as an example the interview he did with Mother Teresa for the BBC, and he describes meeting her as one of the greatest blessings of his life.

Alongside those who reject cultural forms are thinkers and activists who do not isolate religion from culture or reject its institutions. For such theologians or artists, religion has the inherent power to invigorate and transform experience at all levels.

---

[7] Malcolm Muggeridge, *Christ and the Media* (Grand Rapids, MI: Eerdmans, 1977), p. 30.

[8] *Ibid.*, p. 68.

The Making of Meaning

At the same time, they believe that humanly created symbols—in all the arts and sciences—introduce multiple languages and thought structures through which faith may be communicated. They see faith and culture engaged in continuous dynamic relationships; thus there is a dual affirmation of both. For many in the Judaic-Christian tradition this positive view of culture is rooted in an irreducible confidence in the goodness of creation, and they approach its mystery with awe and wonder. They discern the continuity of this creation throughout time and liken human inventiveness to the work of a creator God. Such a point of view would reject the Muggeridge contentions that television is innately corrupting medium.

Significant conflicts, nevertheless, may arise from what is seen as a positive interplay of faith and culture. There is a dark side to human creativity. People disfigure their lives, their works, other creatures, society, and the earth itself. Thus while affirming the goodness of creation and its continuous overflow into human experience, as one surveys the destructive dimensions of human creativity, one feels a bewildering, almost overwhelming, despair. The resulting tensions are endured only through faith in an ever-present possibility of redemption and renewal.

Seen from this perspective the mass media, like other cultural creations, are inherently positive. At the same time, realism is important; understanding human corruption modifies our attitudes about the worth of what we create, and television must be included. Like all cultural forms, media images are continually subject to self-aggrandizement and must be open to transformation and renewal. An affirmative, yet realistic, view of culture may drive transformers of culture to seek interactive, dynamic relationships between communication technologies and faith.[9]

Remaking Meanings

Churches that would be innovative in using communication technology must understand what the media do well in our religiously plural society. Television, for example, is made for mythologies, stories that help us to understand ourselves, our values, and the events that impinge upon our lives. Without the ideological saturation of television it is hard to imagine how we would elect politicians, maintain the vast socio-ecomonic system in which millions of individuals are enmeshed, or make choices about the environment. Despite the disdain of some intellectuals and religious groups, it has become a fabricator of public meanings and designer of images that foster confidence and faith in institutional policies. The mythologies that promote and reinforce the American Way are found in the familiar commercials, news programs, sit-coms, press conferences, sports, and soaps.

Just as the apostle at Ephesus threatened the economic well-being of the silversmiths who marketed popular images of the goddess Artemis, Paul's contemporary counterpart who questioned our symbol system would threaten our concept of the good life and put many of us out of business.

Do denominations have any radically different stories to tell? Since a vast, complex communication system—encompassing radio, print, computers, and television—is necessary to maintain our way of life and foster confidence in it as well, it is not at all clear that religious groups in America really want to offer any mythologies that run counter to a public faith. Are American

---

[9] See Niebuhr, *Christ and Culture*, for an overview of attitudes about the relationships between faith and culture.

The Making of Meaning

churches and synagogues so comfortably situated underneath the canopy of the American Way that their traditional myths seem irrelevant, insignificant, or unimportant? Certainly the messages of conservative denominations blend rather unobtrusively with the prevailing political ideology that has dominated American society over the last ten years. While they represent a diversity of liturgical rites and beliefs, some churches espouse values which are indistinguishable from those of a larger public religion. On the other hand, if there are faith claims and loyalties that do not fit well under this canopy, how are alternative stories told? And where? To whom? In a country where religious freedom prevails, denominations are free to produce and circulate their own myths and principles of faith. The rapid growth of VCR technology and cable makes available new channels of audio-visual communication.

The efforts of religious groups today to use communication technology may be compared with those of small, isolated cults in the pre-Constantinian era seeking to utilize the arts practiced in Greco-Roman culture. At that time Christians, Jews of the Diaspora, and followers of various cults coexisted under the overarching dominion of the Roman empire. As we saw at Dura-Europos, they modified the language and code of the visual arts to suit their own faith and liturgical rites. Except during periods of persecution, many different religions could pick and choose among a variety of classical forms and symbols, transforming and adapting them according to local faith, customs, and indigenous styles. Similarly in the United States today, under the encompassing domain of a public religion, diverse religious groups may select and modify communications to suit their faith and practice. Acknowledging loyalty to the civil order that provides stability and a primary frame of meaning, modern churches and synagogues, like those of the pre-Constantinian era, learn to live with dual and sometimes competing values.

The reverse side of the media's capacity to frame shared beliefs and embody symbols of a public faith is their power to de-mystify, to undo meaning, and shake up commonly held assumptions. Alongside the iconifying power of the media is their capacity to become iconoclastic. In religious terms this suggests that, in addition to its priestly role of confirming belief, communications technology today can be used in a prophetic way. Historically the prophets in Israel called the nation back to its basic principles. They boldly and fiercely drew attention to the defections of a nation under God and the social ills which had overtaken society. A prophetic strain has continued in Christianity which attempts to judge social institutions and critique culture in light of its principles.

Now we may ask, can a prophetic critique be made of public religion and its symbols purveyed though the mass media? We have seen how TV's sit-coms, soaps, dramas, and commercials may be a source of shared myths reinforcing our corporate dream. Are there those in the media or elsewhere willing to abandon the role of priest and assume the responsibility of prophet?

We have learned through polls that Americans generally expect the press to play a critical role in a democratic society, monitoring authoritative institutions and individuals so that power is not abused and the freedom of choice in our corporate life is genuinely free. In 1986 an extensive investigation, sponsored by the *Los Angeles Times-Mirror* and conducted by the Gallup Organization, indicated that the public expected newspersons and institutions—more than government, business, or labor unions—to be truthful and fulfill a fundamental obligation to the public as watchdog in an open, democratic society. The entire spectrum of respondents—men and women, rich and poor, young and old, Democrats and Republicans—believed that the media should serve as a watchdog. A number of critics today, however, believe that journalists have become so closely

The Making of Meaning

identified with economic-political establishments that they have ceased to keep a watchful eye on them.

An investigative journalist, Mark Hertsgaard, for example, concludes that the press has become so much a part of the establishment that it has failed to make us aware of many issues affecting the public good. The situation will only get worse, he says, unless "the men and women of the press return to first principles and live up to the concept of a free and independent press first upheld some two hundred years ago by the American Revolution."[10] From the basic commitments of the prophetic tradition emerges a concern for justice and compassion. Both journalist and prophet, however, begin with the essential question on which ethical and value choices turn: "What is going on?" In seeking to discover the truthful circumstances surrounding events, they provide information that enables people to evaluate situations and decide on a course of action. The eighth-century prophets made their judgments only after a penetrating look at what was going on around them, describing how the righteous were sold for silver and the heads of the poor were trampled into the dust.

Recent criticism of the media in the United States has focused on their neglect in bringing to light issues that might affect evaluation and decision-making. A communications professor at Sonoma State University has for twelve years collected major stories that were underreported in the United States. Among the top ten for 1987 were the Reagan administration's attempt to limit press access to government documents, governmental support of biological warfare research in univer-

---

[10] Mark Hertsgaard, *On Bended Knee: The Press and the Reagan Presidency* (New York: Farrar, Straus & Giroux, 1988), p. 349.

sity laboratories, the documentation of worldwide nuclear accidents, and the dumping of toxic wastes abroad, particularly in Third World countries.[11]

The world beyond our family and neighborhood is, and always has been, a symbolic world, where institutions, far-away lands, and calamitous events are "known" primarily through the symbolic form we now call "news." Yet the quality of the rain that falls on our fields and the air which we and our immediate neighbors breathe are affected by the principalities and powers perceived primarily through mass media. If we are to exercise any freedom of choice about the larger whole of which we are a part, it is critically important to question vigorously the makers of meaning and the truths they have selected to construct the "world" and its "events." If decisions, conservative or liberal, are to have any significance, a free flow of information is essential. Otherwise, there is no genuine choice; nor is there any chance for prophetic judgment.

Churches, synagogues, and concerned individuals who wish to understand and challenge the formulation of these symbolic worlds need only select and scrutinize the reporting of particular events. In the process they may be able to begin to distinguish between the massive, entangled flux of experience and those representations deliberately chosen and presented to answer the fundamental question: "What is going on?" A discussion might focus, for example, on the disastrous oil spill in the Alaskan waters on Good Friday, March 24, 1989, and critically analyze the reports of that event. Since these may eventually become the basis of our political and economic decisions about oil exploration and the environment, it is important to understand how the reporting of the event shaped our perceptions at the time.

---

[11] Craig McLaughlin, "Project Censored: Ten Stories the Daily Press Missed—and Why," *San Jose Metro* (August 16–22, 1988), pp. 9-10.

The Making of Meaning

Many controversies surround environmental policies and such discussions could highlight the importance of symbolic construction for a wide range of religious and secular interests.

If, for instance, one reviews the tapes of commercial and public television during the week following the disaster, several types of images can be detected. Many video sequences were shot from a helicopter, for example, keeping viewers at a distance from the blackened shoreline and waters of Prince William Sound. Then for prolonged periods of time public and network television showed interviews with oil company officials, members of Congress, the governor of Alaska. One saw tight shots—talking heads—debating the merits and failures of various containment strategies. President Bush's telecast press conference brought in members of his administration who had been there and helped to determine clean-up procedures. In addition, reporters packaged small vignettes, human interest segments featuring fisherman and villagers whose livelihood and way of life was facing destruction. Countless charts and maps pinpointed the area and then identified, through color diagrams, the path of the drifting oil. Following the reports of the alleged drunken state of the ship's captain were stories and pictures about him. The judge who first set bail for Joseph Hazelwood described the oil spill as the worst environmental disaster since Hiroshima.

Yet if we review the dominant images provided through television coverage, it becomes clear that viewers were not permitted an unflinching view of the appalling destruction of the pristine environment. The connecting thread running through almost all of the visual images was, rather, a distancing from death.

Only occasionally, and in less than a split second, could one actually see the painful details of a desecrated nature. There was little or no prolonged camerawork that brought viewers deeply into the horror of the creeping crude oil as it smothered rocks and entombed struggling birds and mammals. It seemed as if anything more than the swiftest glance at such death would be too evocative, too explosive, and would inflame the environmental passions of the public. Even rescue work on stricken creatures was presented only in very small segments. In newspapers one saw only a few photographs of dead birds pulled from beneath the deadly layer of oil or an occasional picture of a group of sea otters besieged by the spill. But these were black and white still photos.

The most graphic descriptions of the death and suffering were verbal. On public radio, for instance, reporters described the truckloads of mammals and birds which were killed outright or had died despite their attempted rescue. No such images appeared on TV. Only public television reported that the Coast Guard had restricted the media in the early days of the spill, and this special story showed some of the scenes of death that authorities had apparently not wanted journalists to visit or describe for readers and viewers. In totalitarian countries, the government may attempt to alter "reality" by absolute censorship of information, sometimes imprisoning and killing those who remember. Yet before the total blackout of news by Chinese authorities, the raw violence suffered by protesters in Tiananmen Square was far more graphic and accessible to TV viewers than the violence inflicted on the Alaskan wildlife and environment by the oil spill. Even in a free society, powerful institutions may try to buy silence, offering financial incentives to those who forget or shut their eyes. A PBS broadcaster reported via radio that the oil company had contracted with Alaskan fisherman and paid them to not take media representatives out on their boats or even talk to them. Somewhat later ABC News reported that Alaskans were being hired at $16.69 per hour to clean up the environment—with the stipulation that they were not to talk to anyone in the media.

The Making of Meaning

The apparent restriction of information about the Alaskan oil spill is somewhat analagous to the blackout of independent reporting of the Granada invasion. Persons in positions of power have learned from the Vietnam experience that the portrayal of suffering, especially the suffering of the innocent, may be revolutionary, far too dangerous to bring to the public forum of television. Although Alaskans reacted with anger and resentment, a further complication lay in the fact that the stricken port city was awash with money. Will this dim the Alaskans' memories of their oily wasteland?

Viewers, even those who stop to raise questions about the symbolic pictures presented, have fragile memories. There are critics, in fact, who argue that the news helps us more to forget than to remember. The media, observes Fredric Jameson, a professor of Literature and History of Consciousness at Santa Cruz, may serve as agents and mechanisms for our historical amnesia as they systematically relegate recent historical experience into the past.[12] Disasters, both natural and human, the rise and fall of regimes, crucial events that seem for a moment to define or destroy a people—all seem to be daily wiped away from memory. Few seem to care about prolonged memories or sustained questions about the present and future—in Alaska or anywhere else. A prophetic critique of the media might well begin with the moral imperatives to get stories straight, and to remember. On such frail, human efforts hinge many ethical and political decisions.

In addition to keeping a watchful eye on the news, groups in churches might also discuss media symbols of the good life and compare them with those from their own religious tradition. In

---

[12] Fredric Jameson, "Postmodernism and Consumer Society," *The Anti–Aesthetic: Essays on Postmodern Culture* Hal Foster, Ed. (Port Townsend, WA: Bay Press, 1983), p. 125.

Judaism and Christianity, the problem of suffering—individual and communal—is paramount. That insoluble, unbearable mystery of existence weaves its way through biblical narratives and the psalms. In the eucharist, Christ's passion is central. Yet in our day-to-day symbolic world, the litanies of a consumer society—the commercials—banish suffering altogether or resolve pain in a matter of seconds. Except for the "ouch" that brings out a band-aid or the stuffy nose that prompts a cold remedy, people in commercials are in an eternal state of freedom and happiness. The good life is identified largely by the consumption of particular products.

To whom are these litanies of the good life addressed? If we look at products that are advertised most frequently in magazines, newspapers, and on television, we will find that the vast spectrum of consumer goods and services is directed primarily to middle and lower income groups. Watching an evening of television one sees mainly affordable and accessible items—food, beverages, insurance, cosmetics and personal items, household goods and appliances, home improvement and financing, over-the-counter medicines, bargain travel packages, and automobiles. Occasionally high-priced luxury items are advertised, but persons who command the most wealth in this country are not the targets of commercials. Instead, more than one hundred billion dollars are spent to encourage those with less money to spend more and more in pursuit of the good life and in the exercise of their "freedom."

In our society, the values of liberty and individuality are symbolized primarily in material terms. As John F. Wilson has observed, there is very little asceticism in American culture, even though in other societies that spiritual discipline is an important

The Making of Meaning

means of exercising individual liberty.[13] Have American religious groups uncritically adopted the media symbols of freedom and the good life, allowing their own to slip into the shadows? The systematic blackout of suffering and the quick, short-term solution to pain may have so deeply permeated our TV consciousness that the insoluble, blurred dimensions of human distress are unmanageable and overwhelming. Our most pervasive cultural symbols tell us that there is twenty-four-hour relief for pain.

In focusing upon the latent religious function peformed by mass media today, I have emphasized the power of contemporary communications technologies, underwritten by institutional sponsors, to construct images of authority. The purpose has been to draw attention to the symbolic worlds we enter when we go beyond the boundaries of everyday routines and try to think about our corporate life. Prior to the information revolution, public symbols that bridged personal and communal experience were located in city squares and cathedrals. Today, access to our abstract, larger "world" is found in mass media, as we read the newspaper, switch on the radio, turn on the TV. Like medieval peasants who left their fields to gape at pictures in stone and glass authorized by the church authorities, we depend on institutional images to explain the larger system to which we belong.

In this section I have tried to suggest ways that concerned churches and individuals may try, even momentarily, to step outside of the symbolic atmosphere that surrounds us, asking first of all if there are any alternative mythologies. Second, I have indicated the need for a prophetic watch over the making of meaning by the media and over the symbolic forms that pur-

---

13 John Wilson, *Public Religion in American Culture*, p. 115.

port to explain "how things are." Many congregations, however, may have little or no desire to take on either task. To conservative religious groups a critique of symbols constructed by the media might be seen as unpatriotic, not prophetic. With a realignment of religious loyalties within and across denominations, persons concerned with questions of theology and the environment, for example, may actually find greater empathy and interest *outside* of the church.

Now we turn to consider another role that images have played, particularly in the context of religious ritual. The principal role of religion has been to offer individuals a way out of suffering and provide rites which enable them to return to reality with hope and courage. As we saw earlier, the high arts have increasingly played a redemptive role for many people who turn to the arts to construct personal meanings and find fulfilment. We want now to examine this challenge to the churches.

High Art: The Making of Private Meanings

Most educated Americans are appreciative of "Art." For certain types of people it outclasses motherhood and apple pie in reverence and approval. Furthermore, as we have seen, the creative act of making images and objects has, for some artists, taken on ritualistic overtones. In this section I would like to consider those aspects of high art which may be compared to the saving dimensions of religion in satisfying the personal need for meaning. For this spiritualization of art presents a special challenge to religious communities, particularly those which have traditionally emphasized liturgy and the sacraments.

Religious rituals have always enabled individuals to withdraw from ordinary life and to experience some kind of self-transcendence. One then returns to everyday reality with renewed energy and hope. This self-surpassing dimension of religious ritual has been rediscovered in artistic creation. During our century, the quests of spiritually inclined artists have altered not

The Making of Meaning

only the content and form of religious symbols, but also their function and location. Theological concerns—the knowledge of God, the world, and authentic human experience—may today be pursued through art. Adventures of the spirit once associated with religious faith and rites have been gradually transposed by artists from religion to artistic creation. As the expression of an individual spiritual quest, art-making is transfigured into personal salvation. In their passionate engagement with the making of images and objects, some artists achieve a sense of transcendence, fulfilling, to a degree, the human desire for "something else" beyond the self. In this respect the practice of art has tended to fulfill human needs once met by religion.

If we look through artists' diaries, notes in sketchbooks, reported conversations, letters, and journals we can construct a rough profile of some of the inner dynamics of the creative processes. Obviously artists work and think about their activity in quite different ways, and an attempt to sort out and organize the variable motifs is at best approximate. Still, even a crude sketch of aesthetic passions may help us better understand how art may become a substitute for religious experience. By clustering, for example, some of the elements of artistic production— transformation, order, play, the construction of another world— we can compare the inner dynamics to the rhythm of religious ritual. Although the liturgical drama of ritual is missing, we can detect similar patterns of withdrawal, transformation and return.

Among these elusive processes of creativity are the experience of transformation, the awareness of the human capacity and pleasure in creativity (that drive associated with bringing something into being which did not previously exist), the ability to envision order and wholeness, the demands of discipline, and the joy of play. In various ways, these elements may separate and recombine; from time to time they result in a sense of self-transcendence. This interplay of physical, mental, and spiritual actions enables artists to create and to live in another world, one which Ernest Becker describes as a "second" world, a world of humanly created meaning, a new reality. That creative illusion, he says, is "life itself to the symbolic animal."[14]

To understand fully the challenge to the religious imagination, we need to look at these and other elements of artistic activity in greater detail. Yet the selection of one or two illustrates the spiritual lure of the practice of art. The sense of transformation, for example, is one of the most clearly articulated elements in artistic experience. Artists witness on many levels to their revisioning of the world. It is not, as Paul Klee has said, the business of art to render the visible, but to *render visible*. Looking at hundreds of drawings and paintings produced by Vincent Van Gogh in the last eighteen months of his life fills viewers with wonder as they marvel at his impassioned, transforming vision. Moreover, over the centuries literature has recorded radically changed views of the world. A prototypical transformation is described by Plato in the parable of the cave. A prisoner, once unchained and exposed to the light of the sun, upon returning to the cave can never again see as reality the shadows cast on the wall. Centuries later, William James described the marvelously transfigured world of twice-born individuals.

It is in these self-forgetful moments of creation and construction that art is ritualized. Painters may lose all sense of time. To shape, to change, to make sketches, throw them out and start over, to design, make choices, refine, and finally to say the work is as complete as one can make it—these are typical moments of creation. Etienne Gilson, in *Painting and Reality*, emphasizes the profound joy of creation. Yet, he says, those who create will find

---

[14] Ernest Becker, *The Denial of Death* (New York: The Free Press, 1973), p. 189.

The Making of Meaning

themselves "in contact with the closest analogue there is, in human experience, to the creative power from which all beauties of art as well as those of nature ultimately proceed. Its name is Being."[15] While such exhilarating moments of creativity are not, of course, exclusively the province of art, we sometimes accept them as such—especially in a secular society where traditional rituals have often become lifeless and perfunctory.

Artists and appreciative viewers who are disenchanted with historical religious traditions, confess to art's mystical and mysterious transformations, claiming for it a special kind of revelation. Mircea Eliade has detected in such claims "myths of the elite," and he points out certain "survivals" and "camouflages" of ritual and myth in modern society. Artists, along with critics and wealthy patrons, proclaim a special kind of knowledge—or "gnosis." It has the advantage, he says, of "being at once spiritual and secular in that it opposes both official values and the traditional churches."[16] Nevertheless, Eliade recognizes art as a creative, transformative escape from the ordinariness and pain of a secular society that seems to have lost all sense of wonder and mystery.

Mainline religious denominations must understand the ways in which the arts satisfy the human need for transformation and mystery. Only then will they realize why so many have looked outside of institutional religion for the renewal and nurture of the life of the spirit. Critical inquiry and appreciation will indicate for them both likenesses and differences between religious and aesthetic experiences, and a clearer grasp of the analogies may enable churches to recover the symbolic enrichment which the arts bring to worship.

---

15 Etienne Gilson, *Painting and Reality* (New York: Meridian Books, 1961), p. 275.

16 Mircea Eliade, *Myth and Reality*, trans. Willard R. Trask (New York: Harper & Row, 1963), p. 189, 190.

Some of the most profound differences come to light when we scrutinize the nature of transcendence and the metaphysical dimensions of religious ritual. With artistic activity—as with intense engagement in sports—there may be such encompassing involvement that, conscious only of a flow of activity, one loses a sense of self. Entirely engrossed in the immediacy of time and action, one "transcends" ordinary boundaries; everything is left behind. Both artists and athletes have testified to a temporary loss of ego and to a sense of vitality more rewarding than the finished object or the winning of the game.

Transcendence in religious ritual and meditation also involves a self-forgetfulness or loss of ego-centeredness. Participants in liturgy escape the bonds of time and space and transcend the boundaries of individual consciousness and conditions, fulfilling the human desire for "something more" and the urge to counter the suffering and death that are part of life. For worshippers, transcendence is a state of being through which they are able to rise above pain, futility, and a sense of impermanence, achieving if only momentarily an awareness of an "other" realm or being. The essentially saving dimension of religion can be found in the sacred literature of world religions. There, sociologist of religion Bryan Wilson notes, are accounts of human anxiety and anguish and of ways to assuage these experiences. All religions, he says, provide a vocabulary of sufferings—personal, societal, and universal—and prescribe beliefs and practices for their relief.[17] While symbolism and expression vary among diverse faiths, practices, and ethical action, all cultures and religions offer reassurance and the prospect of salvation.

---

[17] Bryan Wilson, *Religion in Sociological Perspective*, p. 31.

The Making of Meaning

Devotional figures such as Christ, Mary, or the Buddha frequently serve as concrete symbols through which persons in prayer or contemplation achieve a sense of the Other. In the mystical traditions of both Christians and Jews one often finds the image of a ladder of ascent; with each rung one moves further away from the familiar surroundings of the everyday world into a different realm of consciousness. To some mystically inclined individuals the One to whom they ascend is wholly other and nameless, while Jews and Christians draw upon biblical metaphors such as Father, Lord, Creator, Judge, and Redeemer to describe the One with whom they seek communion. Today feminist theologians question many of these metaphors, which impose a culturally conditioned name upon what ultimately defies naming. Yet they too may designate the goal of the search for transcendence as Mother, Earth, or Friend. While theologians differ in the metaphors used to describe the holy, they share the conviction that the "something" symbolized—the aim of mystical longing—is a fundamental reality and not merely a projection of the human imagination. Although devotional practices may often entail the use of art forms, religious transcendence is distinguished from aesthetic transformation by this restless metaphysical desire for an Other.

In churches, liturgical ritual is an occasion for transcendence and for communion with the holy. Through participation in rites and prayers believers affirm the presence of the divine; they are enabled to withdraw from the ordinary world and to experience renewal and a mysterious confirmation of being. The palpable elements of bread and wine of the eucharist are symbols of metaphysical mysteries. Through these sacraments, participants move beyond their immediate human condition and share in Christ's suffering, death, and resurrection. Even though Protestants and Catholics differ in interpretation and emphasis, they share theological assumptions about the revelations of God in Christ and the abiding presence of the Holy Spirit among the faithful.

Also shared by diverse traditions is the corporate nature of salvation. While the experience of transformation is personal, religious rites have confirmed a community as well as the individuals within it. The ritualistic dimensions of art-making, in contrast, are generally experienced by the artist in the seclusion of a studio. There, in direct engagement with clay, wood, or paint, an artist may fulfill to some degree a sense of harmony with these earthy materials and enjoy a release from the tedium of ordinary life through the pleasures of creation. Some artists, seeking to breaking their isolation, included others in these creative, quasi-ritualistic activities during the artistic "happenings" of the 70s or through environmental art projects. The latter often required the participation of a particular community over a period of time.

Christo's "Running Fence" is an example. In his design the artist called for an extended structure which would call attention both to the environment and to human artifacts as they alter and enhance nature. To construct the miles of fence over the California terrain called for the efforts of many individuals, and the process soon took on a life of its own. Although Christo's work has called attention to communal involvement, his grandiose projects—often costing millions—have also met with skepticism. Environmentalists have found him insensitive to ecological concerns, while other critics claim that his flamboyant site sculptures frequently ignore the nature of a community. Art critic Eleanor Munro points out, for example, that "many among Sonoma and Marin counties' economically

The Making of Meaning

pressed and ecologically aware" did not find in the work the "unarguable value" that some in the art world found.[18]

In the absence of shared values and myths, how can a work of art express corporate religious meaning? We recall that the landscapes of inspired painters such as Durand and Inness, as well as the visionary abstractions of Kandinsky, Mondrian, Rothko, and Newman, were expected to communicate universal religious insight. Yet the power of such art to disclose meaning or channel the emotions of others has generally depended upon solitary and subjective interpretations. Inspired landscapes or abstractions may evoke in viewers a sense of wonder, but they leave us to our personal, isolated spiritual meanderings. The breadth and indeterminacy of these epiphanies may be both their strength and weakness, especially in a world skeptical of traditional icons and rituals. It is clear that, unlike film or the performing arts, the visual arts have led us toward private contemplation rather than a corporate or participating ritual experience.

Still, works by inspired abstract painters have helped to transform museums into public shrines, a sacred site for a secular society, particularly for educated urban classes. Those attuned to the spiritual life, but uncomfortable in churches or synagogues, stand side by side with other pilgrims who are making their Sunday trip to the Metropolitan or the Boston Museum of Fine Arts. Indeed, the presentation of some modern masters suggests a chapel-like atmosphere.

In the East Wing of the National Gallery in Washington, D.C., the paintings of Rothko are in a spacious room all to themselves. There is a reverential silence as viewers stand before these simple, elegant paintings which invite them to lose

---

[18] Eleanor Munro, *Originals: Women Artists* (New York: Simon and Schuster, 1979), p. 51.

themselves in the rich overlays of color. Nearby is a room even more liturgical in tone, Newman's "Stations of the Cross." Here visitors proceed from station to station around the circular room much as the faithful followed the biblical stories at Vézelay. There are, of course, obvious differences. While the fourteen stations are numbered, the viewer finds no story except the titles of the paintings and their arrangement in sequential order. In the large rectangular forms, white predominates; in some, the natural tone of the linen canvas provides the light ground. Within the paintings are variations of Newman's familiar "zip," a thin black vertical form that runs from the top to the base of each painting. Some viewers may seek metaphorical connections to traditional Christian symbols suggested in the titles. Collectively, however, the works seem to compel viewers to empty the mind of all figural associations. Those aware of Newman's interest in mysticism may see these as variations of the theme of emptiness, a procession that leads us along the *via negativa*. The final painting, following the Fourteenth Station, has the same general format. But it introduces the only color in the room, a brilliant orange zip on the left side of the painting. Its title is "Be II."

If museums have become holy places in a technological society, the devotions practiced there are purely individual. Unlike ritual spaces of world religions, there are no corporate prayers or communal ritual action. Still, the artists' quests for meaning through the arts may encourage religious groups to rethink their own uses of visual symbols in the liturgical context.

The Church and the Artist

Religious groups sensitive to our society's rediscovery of ritual and spirituality through the arts may also draw artists into the life of the community. At the same time, painters, sculptors, printmakers, and designers, aware of the importance of universal, shared meanings, could be challenged to revitalize tradi-

The Making of Meaning

tional liturgical spaces and symbols. Since artists of the twentieth century have, for the most part, worked independently of institutions, this task of mediating meanings is complex and difficult. In today's diverse and religiously plural world, the racial, ethnic, social, and political differences among congregations are significant. Therefore discussions between artists and religious groups can be initiated and nurtured most effectively within particular, local congregations. This does not, of course, preclude broader and farther-reaching efforts on the part of artists and denominational leaders, but it is not necessary to wait for that to happen. If local churches contact working artists in their area, interaction could bring fresh insights and a renewal of relationships between artist and public. Both artists and congregations would have to be willing to enter into a collaborative, searching process.

Congregations near urban centers, colleges, and universities are likely to find a variety of artists working in diverse materials and styles. Active church persons interested in the arts could take the initiative to meet them, get to know their work, and explore the possibilities of introducing it into liturgical settings. This would be possible even for those Protestant traditions which have rejected images. In the museum we have experienced the meditative tone inspired by some abstract paintings, such as those of Rothko and Newman; similarly, non-representative work could be introduced into worship spaces. Painters, sculptors, and glassmakers working with non-figural forms, in collaboration with knowledgable laypersons, could find modest yet innovative ways to express and transform the aniconic aesthetic we saw in Cistercian churches. The spiritual odyssey frequently undertaken solely by the artist could thus be shared with others. Those who worship will join that spiritual journey as they experience light, color, and the ordering of shapes and form. Thus in the liturgical setting, the works become the occasion not simply for individual meditation, but for shared worship and celebration.

Dialogue can become a common adventure when artist and congregation together explore the possibilities of enriching liturgical space. Usually people defer to the solitary imagination of the artist, but in my experience to do so is partial and misleading. I will take the next few pages to describe what I have learned about the power of the corporate imagination. When I worked over a period of two years with the rabbi and congregation of B'nai Temple Israel, in Monroe, Louisiana, we arrived at a design that I could not have achieved alone.

Commissioned to design mosaic panels for the east wall of the sanctuary, forty feet in length, I consulted first with the rabbi and members of the building committee. As a preparatory step we met often to reflect upon the symbols of faith that were most valued by the congregation. As our discussions continued, these leaders gradually agreed that the major themes were *praise, covenant, justice,* and *lamentation.* This gave me the symbolism to work with. Then I began to experiment with design concepts and materials which might give visual form to these intangibles. At the same time, we began to discuss the work with all the different groups within the congregation.

During this period I recalled the ideas expressed by art historian Edgar Wind in an essay, "Art and the Will."[19] He pointed to times in history when artist and patron have creatively worked together. Yet, he contended, we still cling to the romantic notion that artists are singularly alone and produce only as the spirit moves them. Fearing that we might disturb the artist's imagination, we allow important decisions—the symbolic themes, context, and purpose—to be made by one person

---

[19] Edgar Wind, "Art and the Will," *Art and Anarchy* (New York: Random House, 1969), pp. 88-89.

The Making of Meaning

alone. To illustrate the creative process, Wind found the temple and its forecourt an appropriate metaphor. In the forecourt, he wrote, the artist should not be left alone; this is the place for interaction and discussion with others. Only afterwards does the artist withdraw alone into the recesses of the temple.

When I was experimenting with sketches for this project, combining, recombining, ordering and reordering colors, lines, shapes and tones, I was aware of the genuinely solitary dimensions of the creative process. Working through seemingly infinite sequences of visual possibilities, the artist is quite alone. My responsibility was to explore rigorously all the many ways the fundamental symbols chosen by the congregation could best be expressed. What materials? What formal relationships? How to compose for the given space? What new ways of visualizing traditional meanings?

As I deliberated with the congregation about theological symbols, I began to work simultaneously on the Hebrew alphabet, studying the letters for their formal and symbolic qualities. I wanted to explore their inherent beauty and expressive character as a basis for the overall design. Many scholars have drawn attention to the poetic and mystical significance of Hebrew as a liturgical language. Rabbi Lawrence Kushner, for example, has pointed out that the characters are not simply signs for sounds:

> They are symbols whose shape and name, placement
> in the alphabet, and words they begin, put them
> each as the center of a unique spiritual constellation.
> They are themselves holy. They are vessels carrying
> within the light of the Boundless One.[20]

Mindful of this mystical sense, I became convinced that the design for the large rectangular wall should feature Hebrew

---

[20] Lawrence Kushner, *The Book of Letters: A Mystical Alef–bait* (New York: Harper & Row, 1975), p. 5.

characters. But how? In what kind of composition? I began to organize the letters of the words, *praise, covenant, justice,* and *lamentation,* into clusters of geometric shapes, trying out various styles of Hebrew characters. In the midst of this intensive, isolated period, I showed some of the compositions to a friend, a young architect from Israel. I began to discuss the project with him, selecting the design I thought strongest and most fitting for the space. He liked the design very much, but I remember most vividly his additional remarks: "Hebrew is a musical, poetic language. The four words you are using—praise, covenant, justice, and lamentation—almost ask to be joined together in a phrase." His comments instantly triggered an idea that had been forming intuitively in my mind. "That's it!" I exclaimed. "We'll turn the whole wall into a song of praise and lamentation." From the Psalms we selected two phrases that include the four chosen symbolic themes. The congregation was enthusiastic.

From that time the design process took an unexpected turn. I started afresh, but now with a clear sense of what must be accomplished. Hebrew characters fashioned in gold tesserae would be placed individually on rectangular panels of marble mosaic. The panels ranged in tones from pure white to a dark, earth brown. Then all thirty-six panels would be arranged to create a wall of poetry; on the upper level: "Song of love and justice I sing" and below that: "Out of the depths I cry, O Lord." The final panel in the series was pure white, ending the phrase with silence and light alone. At the base of each mosaic panel was placed a small candle. When the panels were finally completed, I knew that the sacramental forms were corporate and historical, not just individual private symbols. The panels were dedicated at Chanukah, the Festival of Lights, and the service concluded with the lighting of the candles. The sanctuary was filled with light and song.

The pluralism and diversity of religious groups today will mean that no one style or aesthetic approach will dominate.

The Making of Meaning

Non-representational art, for example, may be more suitable for certain groups that have steadfastly maintained an aniconic tradition. From the Cistercians we have learned the beauty of the aesthetic of emptiness, based on pure forms, light, and pro-portionality. We know that measure, color, shadows, and voids are visual elements which may be orchestrated to produce eloquent symbolic language. We also know from the two spiritu-alist moderns who pioneered abstraction, Kandinsky and Mondrian, that some artists have found non-representational painting and sculpture to be the most fitting expressions of re-ligious reality. Jewish temples and modern churches wishing to follow aniconic principles could introduce into worship spaces a splendor of light, color, and order which, without recourse to images, could enhance the mystery of faith. On the other hand, religious groups in the iconic tradition might learn from artists who discerned through natural forms a sense of harmony with the universe, or signs of the interconnectedness of all life. We have seen how nature has been a source of wonder and awe for nineteenth and twentieth-century artists like Cole, Allston, and Dove. Churches might seek out those who are exploring the mystery of the natural order and invite them to reshape tradi-tional symbols.

In facing and assessing the challenges of art, congregations need to remember that creation—as idea or experience—is cen-tral to both religion and aesthetics. As we have seen, theologi-ans, artists, and critics have in various ways associated the quest for spirituality with art. One contemporary critic, Suzi Gablik, has called upon artists to recover the human "capacity for tran-scendence, and the visionary role of art for healing culture and opening the heart to meaning."[21] Religious groups that recog-

---

[21] Suzi Gablik, "Reclaiming Sacred Vision," *Art Papers* 10/6 (1986): 4.

nize the spiritual attraction of creative activity may reclaim its inclusive, not exclusive, dimensions. Making a painting, designing a tapestry, forming a vessel are creative, symbolizing acts. So also is the shaping of liturgy, meditating, or doing theology.

Artists and Theologians Meet

In one area the interests of theologians and artists converge: exploring the symbols or metaphors used to express transcendent being. During the twentieth century many artists with explicit religious concerns, as we have seen, simply eliminated visual metaphors from their work, while nineteenth-century artists, no longer working in liturgical settings, transformed landscape into a religious icon. Since the Romantic era, in fact, artists' search for the proper metaphors to express the mystery of being has led them increasingly to share the tasks of philosophers and theologians. Today artists and theologians face similar problems of discerning meaningful symbols for the divine amid fragmented religious institutions and the materialism of our society. In the pluralism of modern life there is no unity of vision and no unquestioned authority to make decisions about symbols. Furthermore, some contemporary thinkers, mindful of our religiously plural world, assert that a major task of theology itself is artistic: the discernment, formulation, and critique of the symbols and metaphors used to characterize the divine-human relationship.

Looking critically at the symbols of faith, theologian Gordon Kaufman deepens our consciousness of the inscrutable mystery within which we live and which we try to name. He underscores the importance of metaphors for God that enable people to grasp what is essentially unknowable. Such symbols are directly related to the ordering and interpretation of human experience. As experience has changed over time, so have the symbolizations of the divine-human order. Thus artists and theologians find common cause in confronting these changes and exploring

The Making of Meaning

new visual metaphors.[22] They ask similar questions: How do Christian and Jewish metaphors for God interact with symbols of other traditions? What are some of the non-traditional metaphors to which artists are directing us? What changes in symbols are called for by feminist and liberation theologians? Do their ventures intersect or mutually enrich each other? Raising these questions suggests a larger task, far beyond the scope of this book. Nevertheless, one example may indicate some directions for interdisciplinary reflections—the powerful and pervasive symbol of God: Creator.

Theologians of diverse religious traditions recognize the primacy of the symbol, Creator. It addresses the fundamental human question of origins which is the subject of religious myths. To many it is a blind spot of life, irreducibly mysterious and known only through speculation or metaphor. Following the Genesis account, Christians, despite the prohibition of the second commandment, enhanced the biblical narrative through pictures. Michelangelo's portrayal of God the Creator brought earlier anthropomorphic visualizations to a dramatic climax. Although stylistic variations followed, artists—from the Mannerists to the Bible illustrators of the nineteenth century—followed the Renaissance artist's model: a handsome, elderly but vigorous, bearded white male. Forcefully and gracefully depicted, he brings light, darkness, the seas, heaven and earth, male and female into being. The theological sophistication of Michelangelo's masterpiece has been recognized and thoroughly studied by art historians. This idealized male image in less sophisticated forms became firmly entrenched as a symbol for the Creator God; only gradually was it abandoned by artists,

---

[22] Gordon Kaufman, "Mystery, Critical Consciousness and Faith," in *The Rationality of Religious Belief: Essays in Honor of Basil Mitchell*, William J. Abraham and Steven W. Holtzer, eds. (Oxford: Clarendon Press, 1987), p. 68.

especially those no longer working with explicit scriptural themes.

During the Romantic period some religiously inclined artists found implicit ways to use the creator metaphor. To them the world, especially the world of nature, implied the presence of a divine ordering and originating being. While representative landscapes dominated nineteenth-century painting, in modern art nature images became abstracted. At the same time, however, few painters expressed any concern for relating their work to the traditional religious idea of creation. Instead, as we saw with Arthur Dove, there were simply references to the "essence" or "force" of nature. While we stand before his abstracton, "Rise of the Full Moon," our religious sensibilities may be awakened. But how? Through a momentary feeling of the ultimate order of life? An imaginary moment of creation? Indeterminate, ambiguous, and evocative, the painting allows viewers to draw from a personal reservoir of faith and experience. Although we may respond to it with a sense of wonder, the "icon" neither narrates a sacred story nor uses a heroic male in depicting creation.

Several twentieth-century artists have chosen feminine symbols of creativity as major motifs in their work—though not all, of course, would assign them theological significance. Some dramatically reformed and broadened the metaphorical power of the mother/child symbol, making it a prime metaphor for both the human and natural order. Kaethe Kollwitz and Henry Moore are two artists who changed our way of seeing this fundamental relationship. In Moore's sculpture, the mother/child metaphor becomes a symbol for the interconnectedness of all life forms. Partly because of her circumstances in the slums of Berlin following World War I, Kollwitz's drawings and prints bring together the fundamental human themes of nurturing and death, portrayed through the mother/child relationship. One of her most forceful works is an etching, *Mother with Dead Child.* One has to look very closely to see that there are really two

The Making of Meaning

figures, not one, in the dark, ovoid mass. Gradually we can detect the solitary figure of a woman who has enfolded in her arms the body of a dead child. Bent and arched over the small body, her form is so mingled with the lifeless child that they seem to be one, defying the separation that death brings.

Many artists have looked back in time, both formally and mythologically, to symbols that prevailed in pre-modern cultures. Lucy Lippard has directed our attention to the abundant reservoir of forms and materials used in earlier societies to symbolize life forces—sacred stones, astronomical markings, ritual spaces, altars, earth gods and goddesses. Before images and objects were "Art," they were essentially the human quest for metaphors to understand life processes. They were in fact necessary for communal attunement to these forces. Beginning with age-old motifs, she traces residual overtones in the symbolism of recent artists who seek to draw contemporary viewers into the constant mysteries of creation, nurture, and finally death.[23]

A feeling of creation's awe and mystery has been thematically addressed by several artists who, by placing objects in outdoor sites, have set up an interplay between humanly constructed symbols and the environment. Many of these earthworks have been inspired by ecological concerns; others represent artists' attempts to strip away the veneer of culture and to relocate art in a larger, more enduring reality. For some there are overtones of archaic sacred sites. The work of sculptor Nancy Holt, for example, directs our attention away from a human to a cosmic scheme. Her elegant works are carefully situated to relate to astronomical measures of time, such as the solstices. Simple forms are aligned so that as the earth rotates, changing patterns of light, shadows, solids, and voids witness the passage of time

---

[23] Lippard, *Overlay*. See especially the introduction.

and season and the rhythms of the universe. While viewers responses may be subjective, Holt's works direct us to the cosmic scheme to which we belong. Artists' repeated emphasis upon the processes of nature parallels the efforts of twentieth-century theologians who have tried to enrich and enlarge the symbolization of creation.

One of these theologians is Sallie McFague, who has explored the religious language of images and metaphors. There are, she writes, impersonal and natural models which express feelings of "awe, fear, exultation, and misery in ways which the more anthropocentric models do not." These are not, however, central in the Judeo-Christian tradition where the dominant model is a "personal God relating to responsible and responsive beings." Yet the impersonal and natural models, found in the language of mystics and the imagery of the Psalms, suggest the heights and depths of relating to the cosmic God.[24] McFague notes how the Christian tradition has narrowed the range of its metaphors and focused on hierarchical, authoritarian, and anthropocentric ones. Certain experiences of ecstasy and awe that cannot be adequately understood in traditional models are more fully expressed in the ocean, the sky, and the earth. McFague challenges us to try to understand the resurrection and ascension as the promise of God to be permanently present, "'bodily' present to us in all places and times of our world." How might we view the world, she asks, if we were to experiment with the metaphor of the universe as God's "body"? In an ecological, nuclear age such a metaphor underscores interdependency and mutuality, empowering a sensibility of care and responsibility toward all life.[25]

---

[24] Sallie McFague, *Metaphorical Theology* (Philadelphia: Fortress Press, 1982), pp. 191-192.

[25] McFague, *Models of God*, p. 60.

The Making of Meaning

Throughout her writing Sallie McFague continually emphasizes the metaphorical nature of all our naming of the ultimate mystery. In her theology she shows how the symbol of the creative and nurturing love of God can be enriched through analogies to mother, father, lover, and friend. Given the nature of the divine-human relationship, we need, she writes, a metaphor which "disorients conventional standards and expectations and reorients us to a new way of being in the world." More than just appropriate, feminine models are necessary for both men and women:

> Specifically, the critical experiences expressed most adequately in these models are ones of rebirth, nurture, unmerited love, security in God alone, compassion, forgiveness, service.[26]

Moreover, our understanding of God's transcendence, she says, will be "worldly."[27] For artists one of the most important aspects of Sallie McFague's theology is her conviction that the world and human relationships give us our meeting place with God. Hers is a sacramental theology which recognizes both the power and fragility of symbols. The visual arts, unlike music or language, are concrete; they occupy space and appeal to many of our senses. For some religious traditions the materiality of art has seemed to be a threat to spirituality, while a sacramental theology, however, recognizes the mysterious unity of flesh and spirit. McFague's metaphorical theology may celebrate, rather than reject, the concreteness of the visual arts and their special capacity to embody and communicate our elusive visions and values. At the same time she is at the forefront of those theolo-

---

[26] McFague, *Metaphorical Theology*, p. 177.

[27] McFague, *Models of God*, p. 185.

gians who realize that some of our symbols—even as they appear in churches, or museums—are inadequate for today's world.

Religious currents in twentieth-century art are deep and varied and will have to be sorted out and related to several theological metaphors. There are some painters, photographers, and sculptors whose works shock and indict our society. As the eighth-century prophets denounced Israel, throughout the twentieth century there have been artists who express judgment on modern society and its pathos. Working in different times and media, Ben Shahn and Leon Golub both confront us with the ethical scope of our actions and portray the victims of our system. In causing us to shudder, they are prophetic in ways that traditional religious institutions have not dared to be. The writings of liberation and feminist theologians may help us gain additional perspective on such artists.

Recognizing the diversity of religious concerns in twentieth-century art, lay persons and theologians may find it an opportune time to draw out and explore the values they share with artists working in their communities. This could have an impact not only upon liturgical art but also upon the public roles that art might play. One role for churches today then, is to join artists in reconsidering the arts as life-enhancing. In particular, theologians and lay leaders can direct our attention to the many ways in which images give tangible form to our faith and ultimate loyalties.

Image and Faith

Throughout this book we have considered the changing functions of images, concluding with particular emphasis on the differences which have arisen between high and popular art in contemporary American culture. Yet in one important way they are indistinguishable. In museums as well as on television, images attest to values and world views. The essential power of images is their capacity to give material form to invisible faith. If

The Making of Meaning

we look back over history, we see an almost endless panorama of symbols human beings have fashioned to impose order on experience—from the handprints on a paleolithic wall to the pervasive electronic images which leap across national barriers and boundaries. Both high and popular art document the human construction of meaning, using material of the seen, known world to interpret experience and to legitimate faith.

Yet in today's world multiple faiths and symbols coexist. Distinguishing faith from religion, H. Richard Niebuhr observed that our whole culture witnesses to a conflict of faiths "distinctly different from the collisions among religions or between religion and irreligion."[28] Faith, according to Niebuhr, is active; it calls forth a commitment of ourselves to something. The contours of contending faiths become clear if we look at the centers of value which inspire our devotion. He has identified a host of Olympian gods that compel our zeal: "our country, our ideologies, our democracies, civilizations, churches, our art which we practice for art's sake, our truth which we pursue for truth's sake, our moral values, our ideas and the social forces which we personalize, adore and on which we depend for deliverance from sheer nothingness and the utter inconsequence of our existence."[29]

Those Olympian gods are even more abundant now than when Niebuhr wrote, and they exert far-reaching influence and power. Transformed by communication technologies, contemporary mass media have become instrumental in a worldwide symbolization of ideologies—social, economic, political. High art also embodies a variety of faiths—in individualism, in private visions, and in the art market. In his disclosure of compet-

---

[28] H. Richard Niebuhr, *Monotheism and Western Culture*, with supplementary essays (New York: Harper & Brothers, 1960), p. 11.

[29] *Ibid.*, p. 120.

ing cultural faiths, Niebuhr has drawn attention to the multiple symbolic worlds that confer meaning on our lives and evoke our deepest loyalties.

For makers, consumers, and interpreters of images, Niebuhr's understanding of faith challenges us to understand the partial truth, even self-aggrandizement, present in our constructions of meaning. The human tendency to turn relative metaphors into absolute ones is present in all cultural forms—high or low. There is much work to be done. Those of us who are concerned with popular culture will need to sift through massive amounts of informational and entertainment material in order to critique the ideologies presented. Observers of high art will need to analyze its cultic and individualistic symbols, its dominant value as an investment commodity, and the general absence of interest in shared, public meanings.

Persons who reflect critically upon our imagistic symbolic worlds may be drawn into what Niebuhr has called a "permanent revolution of the mind and heart," an unguarded adventure of the spirit which opens them to endless new possibilities. Those who take part in this revolution will be called upon to play dual roles as symbol makers and users as well as symbol destroyers—iconifiers and iconoclasts. They will live both within and without Christian faith. As iconifiers, they will understand their power to give visible form to invisible faith. Some may dare to venture into an uncharted sea of being in search of more adequate symbols for our time. Alongside iconifiers are those who believe that no single myth encompasses all. They understand the fragility of symbolic worlds and realize that even as symbols protect and provide us with meaning, they also limit our knowing. Sensitive to the potential of myth to distort, they must at times become daring iconoclasts.

As women and men struggle to discover, to communicate, and to participate in contemporary symbolic worlds of liberation and redemption, superficial distinctions between high and popu-

211

The Making of Meaning

lar art fade. Similarly, iconifiers and iconoclasts join together as they enter into a continuous revolution of faith.

SELECTED BIBLIOGRAPHY

Allston, Washington. *Lectures on Art, and Poems*. Edited by Richard H. Dana, Jr. New York: Baker and Scribner, 1850.

Bagdikian, Ben H. *The Media Monopoly*. Boston: Beacon, 1983.

Bevan, Edwyn. *Holy Images: An Inquiry into Idolatry and Image Worship in Ancient Paganism and in Christianity*. London: George Allen & Unwin, 1940.

_____. *Symbolism and Belief*. Boston: Beacon, 1957.

Bercovitch, Sacvan. *The American Puritan Imagination*. London: Cambridge University Press, 1974.

Berger, Peter. *A Rumor of Angels*. Garden City, NY: Doubleday, 1970.

Berger, Peter and Luckmann, Thomas. *The Social Construction of Reality*. Garden City, NY: Doubleday, 1967.

Chave, Anna. *Mark Rothko*. New Haven: Yale University Press, 1989.

Cohn, Sherrye. *Arthur Dove: Nature as Symbol*. Ann Arbor, MI: UMI Research Press, 1985.

Danto, Arthur C. *The Philosophical Disenfranchisement of Art*. New York: Columbia University Press, 1986.

Dionysius the Areopagite. *The Divine Names and The Mystical Theology*. Translated by C. E. Rolt. London: SPCK, 1972.

Ferguson, Peter. *Architecture of Solitude: Cistercian Abbeys in Twelfth-Century England*. Princeton: Princeton University Press, 1984.

Fustel de Coulanges, Numa Denis. *The Ancient City: A Study on the Religion, Laws, and Institutions of Greece and Rome*. Garden City, NY: Doubleday, 1955.

Garside, Charles. *Zwingli and the Arts*. New Haven: Yale University Press, 1966.

Gilson, Etienne. *The Mystical Theology of Saint Bernard*. Translated by A. H. C. Downes. New York: Sheed & Ward, 1940.

_____. *Painting and Reality*. New York: Meridian Books, 1961.

Gitlin, Todd. *Inside Prime Time*. New York: Pantheon, 1985.

Goethals, M. Gregor T. "A Comparative Study of the Theory and Work of Washington Allston, Thomas Cole, and Horatio Greenough." Ph.D. dissertation, Harvard University, 1966.

Gutmann, Joseph, ed. *The Dura-Europos Synagogue: A Re-evaluation 1932-1972*. Chico, CA: Scholars Press, 1973.

Haskell, Barbara. *Arthur Dove*. Boston: New York Graphic Society, 1975.

Hertsgaard, Mark. *On Bended Knee: The Press and the Reagan Presidency*. New York: Farrar, Straus & Giroux, 1988.

Hess, Thomas B. *Barnett Newman*. New York: The Museum of Modern Art, 1971.

Huizinga, Johann. *The Waning of the Middle Ages*. Garden City, NY: Doubleday, 1956.

Inness, George, Jr. *Life, Art and Letters of George Inness*. New York: The Century Co., 1917.

Jamieson, Kathleen Hall. *Eloquence in an Electronic Age: The Transformation of Political Speechmaking.* New York: Oxford University Press, 1988.

Kandinsky, Wassily. *Concerning the Spiritual in Art and Painting in Particular.* New York: George Wittenborn, 1947.

Kitzinger, Ernest. *Byzantine Art in the Making: Main Lines of Stylistic Development in Mediterranean Art.* Cambridge, MA: Harvard University Press, 1980.

_____. *Early Medieval Art in the British Museum.* London: Trustees of the British Museum, 1963.

Kraeling, Karl H. *The Christian Building.* New Haven: Dura-Europos Publications, 1967.

Langer, Susanne K. *Problems of Art: Ten Philosophical Lectures.* New York: Charles Scribner's Sons, 1957.

Leclercq, Jean. *The Love of Learning and the Desire for God.* Translated by Catherine Misrahi. New York: Fordham University Press, 1961.

Lippard, Lucy. *Overlay: Contemporary Art and the Art of Prehistory.* New York: Pantheon, 1983.

McFague, Sallie. *Metaphorical Theology: Models of God in Religious Language.* Philadelphia: Fortress, 1982.

_____. *Models of God: Theology for an Ecological, Nuclear Age.* Philadelphia: Fortress, 1987.

McLoughlin, William. *Revivals, Awakenings and Reform: An Essay in Religious and Social Change in America, 1607-1977.* Chicago: University of Chicago Press, 1978.

Mondrian, Piet. *Plastic Art and Pure Plastic Art, 1937, and Other Essays, 1941-1943*. New York: Wittenborn, Schultz, 1951.

Muggeridge, Malcolm. *Christ and the Media*. Grand Rapids, MI: Eerdmans, 1977.

Munro, Eleanor. *Originals: Women Artists*. New York: Simon and Schuster, 1979.

Niebuhr, H. Richard. *Christ and Culture*. New York: Harper & Row, 1956.

_____. *Monotheism and Western Culture*. New York: Harper & Brothers, 1960.

Noble, Louis Legrand. *The Life and Works of Thomas Cole*. Cambridge, MA: Harvard University Press, 1964.

Novak, Barbara. *American Painting of the Nineteenth Century: Realism, Idealism, and the American Experience*. New York: Harper & Row, 1969.

Panofsky, Erwin. *Abbot Suger on the Abbey Church of St. Denis and its Art Treasures*. Princeton: Princeton University Press, 1979.

Rodman, Seldon. *Conversations with Artists*. New York: Devin-Adair, 1957.

Rosenblum, Robert. *Modern Painting and the Northern Romantic Tradition: Friedrich to Rothko*. New York: Harper & Row, 1975.

Schudson, Michael. *Advertising, the Uneasy Persuasion*. Basic Books, 1984.

Seuphor, Michel. *Piet Mondrian: Life and Work*. New York: Harry N. Abrams, 1956.

Tillich, Paul. *Christianity and the Existentialists*. New York: Charles Scribner's Sons, 1956.

_____. *Theology of Culture*. New York: Oxford University Press, 1964.

Tuchman, Gaye. *Making News: A Study in the Construction of Reality*. New York: The Free Press, 1978.

Wilson, Bryan. *Religion in Sociological Perspective*. New York: Oxford University Press, 1982.

Wilson, John F. *Public Religion in American Culture*. Philadelphia: Temple University Press, 1979.

Wind, Edgar. *Art and Anarchy*. New York: Random House, 1969.

Wuthnow, Robert. *The Restructuring of American Religion*. Princeton: Princeton University Press, 1989.

INDEX

Cowley Publications is a ministry of the Society of St. John the Evangelist, a religious community for men in the Episcopal Church. Emerging from the Society's tradition of prayer, theological reflection and diversity of mission, the press is centered in the rich heritage of the Anglican Communion.

Cowley Publications seeks to provide books, audio cassettes, and other resources for the ongoing theological exploration and spiritual development of the Episcopal Church and other churches in the body of Christ. To this end, it is dedicated to developing a new generation of theological writers, encouraging them to produce timely, creative and stimulating publications of excellence, and making these publications available widely, reaching both clergy and lay persons.

ABOUT THE AUTHOR

Gregor T. Goethals is the author of
*The TV Ritual: Worship at the Video
Altar*. She is professor of art history at
the Rhode Island School of Design and
is also a free-lance designer.